CARIBBEAN COOKING

CARIBBEAN COOKING

Judy Bastyra

WINDWARD

Acknowledgements

I would like to thank the following people for all their help during the writing of this book: Anne Lynch for working so hard at all hours to test the recipes, Mary Tayleur and Simone Sindermann for typing the manuscript, and my many West Indian friends who gave me advice, inspiration and a number of their favourite recipes: Grania de Gannes, Wendy Gregory, Marie Gurly, Caroline Lewis, John Lloyd, Jennifer Mombru, Suzie Montano, Lady Marjorie Pierre, Lady Enid dos Santos and many others too numerous to mention who have entertained me in their homes over the years. Finally I would like to thank my husband Gilbert, who was responsible for introducing me to the delights of the Caribbean.

House Editor: *Julia Canning*
Editor: *Nicole Foster*
Designer: *Glynis Edwards*
Production: *Richard Churchill*

Photography: *Grant Symon*
Illustrations: *Linda Smith*
Home Economist: *Jane Suthering*
Stylist: *Sue Russell*

Published by Windward, an imprint owned by
W.H. Smith & Son Limited
Registered No. 237811 England
Trading as WHS Distributors,
St John's House, East Street, Leicester LE1 6NE

© Marshall Cavendish Limited 1987

ISBN 0 7112 0465 9

Typesetting by Litho Link Limited, Welshpool

Printed and bound in Italy by L.E.G.O.

CONTENTS

INTRODUCTION
A FLAVOUR OF THE ISLANDS

I first became interested in Caribbean cooking on my honeymoon thirteen years ago. I arrived in Trinidad with my West Indian husband, eager to drink in all the wonderful sights, sounds and tastes of the tropics. I was not disappointed. Everything was more vivid than anything I'd ever seen before – and the food, a myriad of flavours, exotic, spicy and very, very tasty. Now I invite you to share my experiences of the culinary delights of the Caribbean islands.

Ingredients

As with most cuisines in the world, the best food is rarely found in hotels and restaurants but in the homes of the local people. I was fortunate to meet on my first trip a wonderful cook, Alice, who introduced me to some of the basic techniques and ingredients which are used throughout the islands.

The cuisine of the Caribbean can be described as substantial and spicy. It is based around the wide variety of tropical fruits and vegetables that grow on the islands: guavas, bananas, mangoes, limes, oranges, pawpaw, pineapple, coconut, okra, plantain, sweet potatoes, yam, cassava, breadfruit and pigeon peas.

Fish plays a dominant role as there is an abundance to be found in the surrounding waters. Chicken, pork and goat are the most popular meats, being easy to rear in the climate.

Seasoning is the very essence of Caribbean cooking, each separate island having its own special combination of herbs – sive (similar to chives), thyme, spring onion, onion, garlic and a little celery is a typical combination. They are all blended together, sometimes with a little water added and kept in a screw-top jar in the refrigerator to be used as required.

Hot seasoning peppers, or chillies as they are called in some of the islands, are very important in all Caribbean cooking. There are many varieties throughout the islands, some can be quite lethal if used without discretion but when used in moderation they add a distinctive flavour. Spices also, such as ginger, nutmeg, mace, allspice and cinnamon are used to season many of the dishes.

Travelling through the islands one soon finds dishes common to many, though each island usually claims the dish solely as its own. For example the Jamaican Stamp and Go (see page 25) can be found in Martinique and Guadeloupe as acrats de morue or in Puerto Rico as bacalaitos.

Another inter-island speciality is Callaloo (Crab and Spinach Soup, see page 14). This thick spicy soup can be found throughout the Caribbean, changing slightly with each island.

There are certain dishes and food, however, that belong solely to one particular island. Salt Fish and Ackee (see page 32) is found only in Jamaica; fried mountain chicken or crapaud – a large edible frog – is a delicacy particular to the island of Dominica and roti is one of the most popular dishes of Trinidad – a flat Indian bread stuffed with curried goat, chicken, shrimp or vegetables, then folded and eaten as a filling snack.

History of the Islands

The Amerindians

Two thousand years ago the Arawaks and the Caribs, Amerindian tribes originating from Venezuela and Guyana, settled in the islands of the Caribbean. They both hunted, fished and grew crops. The Arawaks, a gentle people, were better farmers than the war-like Caribs, who were adept at hunting.

They ate similar diets of maize, cassava, sweet potatoes, arrowroot, beans and peppers. They gathered wild fruit and caught wild game.

A favourite dish was pepperpot, a mixed meat and vegetable stew. Today pepperpot is made solely with mixed meats, hot pepper and cassareep – the boiled juice of grated cassava. It is said that some pepperpots are kept going for years, with fresh meat being added to the pot every few days, while some are even passed on from generation to generation.

The Europeans

The Spanish: In 1492 Christopher Columbus set sail for the Far East in search of gold and riches for the King and Queen of Spain. When Columbus arrived on Watling Island in the Bahamas in October 1492 he thought he had finally reached the East (or the Indies as it was then known). He stopped briefly on Cuba and then sailed on to Hispaniola (now called Haiti and the Dominican Republic), which was to become the first Caribbean colony of Spain.

In the following years the islands of Cuba, Jamaica and Puerto Rico, which together with Hispaniola make up the Greater Antilles, all became Spanish colonies. To the south in the Leeward and Windward islands there was little Spanish penetration, though a small colony of Spaniards did settle in Trinidad.

The gentle Arawaks were soon exploited by the colonists, who put them to work cultivating their crops, digging for gold and using them as slaves. Within 100 years most of the Arawaks were wiped out, by both war and disease.

These early colonists brought with them many of the fruit and vegetables that we now associate with the Caribbean: limes, oranges, mangoes, bananas, breadfruit, tamarind, ginger, coffee, coconut and sugar cane.

Many Spanish dishes still remain in the Caribbean cooking of today: Escovitch (Marinated Cooked Fish, see page 24), Bacalaitos or Stamp and Go (Salt Cod Fritters, see page 25) and Cocido de Rinones (Kidney Stew, see page 69).

The British and the French: The British and the French soon challenged the supremacy of Spain in the New World and began to claim many of the Lesser Antilles as their own.

St Christopher, also known as St Kitts, was the first English colony to be founded in the Caribbean by Thomas Warner in 1624. A few years later a French buccaneer, Pierre d'Esnambuc, arrived and the English and French agreed to share the island between them. The English went on to colonize Barbados, Nevis, Montserrat and Antigua. The French spread to Martinique, Guadeloupe, Dominica, St Lucia and Grenada.

Barbados in particular has retained much of the British influence. For example, one of the dishes that is traditionally served at Christmas time in Barbados is called jug jug. It is made from a purée of pigeon peas, herbs, salted meats and ground millet, and is supposedly a corruption of haggis, which was originally brought to Barbados by Scottish people in exile there after the Monmouth Rebellion in 1685.

The islands of Guadeloupe and Martinique have remained French. Both are still *départements* of France and as such enjoy a regular supply of French foods, giving the cuisine of these Caribbean islands a mixture of European sophistication and creole spice.

The Dutch: The Dutch were better traders than colonists and colonized only a few small islands which they used primarily as trade depots: Curaçao, Aruba, Saba, St Eustatius and St Martin. They have given the Caribbean one of its most interesting dishes – Keshy Yena (Shrimp-filled Edam Cheese, see page 48) – and the orange-flavoured liqueur Curaçao.

They were also to have a profound influence on Caribbean history through their brief experience of colonization of the rich Brazilian sugar-cane planting area of Pernambuca. Although the Spanish had grown sugar cane imported from plantations in the Canary Islands, it was the Dutch who brought the ideas and technology from Brazil for planting sugar cane on a large scale and making it by far the most profitable crop to produce. The only problem was that it was labour-intensive. There were not enough Amerindians left to work the plantations, so the importation of African slaves began – over fifteen million being imported into the Americas and the Caribbean between 1518 and 1865.

The Africans

When the slaves arrived they brought with them many plants from Africa which still feature strongly

ATLANTIC OCEAN

The Bahamas

Caicos & Turks
Islands

Cuba

G R E A T E R

Cayman Islands

Jamaica

A N T I L L E S

Haiti / Dominican
Republic

Puerto
Rico

Virgin Islands

St Martin

Saba

St Eustatius

St Kitts

Nevis

Antigua

Montserrat

Guadeloupe

Dominica

Martinique

St Lucia

Barbados

St Vincent

Grenada

Tobago

Trinidad

L E S S E R A N T I L L E S

CARIBBEAN SEA

Aruba

Curaçao

in West Indian cooking – pigeon peas, yam, okra and taro. They were given small rations of salt meat and salt fish and supplemented their diet by growing food. Through the creative use of seasoning and spices they evolved a style of cooking characteristic of Caribbean cooking today.

Many of the traditional dishes have survived: Coo Coo (Cornmeal and Okra Pudding, see page 85) and Callaloo (Crab and Spinach Soup, see page 14) are just two examples.

The Indians and the Chinese
By the 1830s when slavery was abolished in many of the islands the system of Indentured Labour was introduced, bringing the East Indians and the Chinese to the Caribbean. They also brought their own culinary expertise with them. Roti, dal puri (puréed split peas), curried goat and Pineapple Spare Ribs (see page 61) have all evolved through their influence.

Creole Cooking
The word 'creole' is synonymous with the Caribbean. It was first used to describe people who were born in the Americas or Caribbean of pure European descent. Today it is more often applied to a person who is of mixed African and European descent. The term creole food is used to describe many of the Caribbean dishes which are of mixed African and European influence.

The Cooking of Today

History has now come full circle with Caribbean people living in many countries all over the world. A few years ago very few people outside the tropics had ever tasted a fresh mango, let alone sampled ackee or breadfruit. All these are now available in many of our local street markets and ethnic shops, giving us the opportunity to learn from Caribbean culture and enjoy a flavour of the islands.

SOUPS

It is surprising how enjoyable a bowl of soup can be whether you live in a hot or cold climate. Nothing goes to waste in a Caribbean kitchen and it is the rich home-made stocks which form the basis of their soups that make them so special. Some of the soups such as Pepper Pot Soup (see page 21) are spicy and substantial, while others like Pumpkin Soup (see page 18) or Chicken Consommé with Peppers (see page 21) make a light appetizing first course.

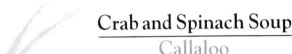

Crab and Spinach Soup
Callaloo

This delicious thick spicy soup is made from taro leaves, okra, coconut and crab meat. The taro leaves grow on a bush that has an edible root called dasheen and rather confusingly, the leaves are known locally as either 'dasheen' leaves or callaloo leaves, after the above dish. However, fresh spinach makes a very good substitute.

Callaloo is found throughout the Caribbean, with each island having its own variation; some have salt pork or bacon which gives a richer stock, while others serve it with the crab claws or the crab meat still in its shell and it is often served as a nourishing meal with the addition of Cornmeal Dumplings (see page 116).

225g/8oz 'dasheen' leaves or 450g/1lb fresh spinach
1 tablespoon butter
1 tablespoon oil
1 onion, finely chopped
2 garlic cloves, crushed
100g/4oz okra, trimmed and sliced
1 fresh chilli, seeded and finely chopped
1 sprig fresh thyme
1 teaspoon finely chopped fresh chives
900ml/1½ pints home-made chicken stock
300ml/½ pint coconut milk (see page 16)
salt and freshly ground black pepper
225g/8oz crab meat, defrosted if frozen
Hot Pepper Sauce (see page 95) (optional)

Serves 6

1 Wash the 'dasheen' or spinach leaves, drain and finely shred.

2 Heat the butter with the oil in a large saucepan over moderate heat, add the onion and garlic and cook for 5 minutes, stirring occasionally, until soft and golden. Add the okra, chilli, thyme and chives and cook for a further 5 minutes, stirring constantly.

3 Stir in the 'dasheen' or spinach leaves and cook for 3 minutes, turning the leaves to ensure they are evenly cooked. Pour over the stock and coconut milk and season with salt and freshly ground black pepper to taste.

4 Bring to the boil, lower the heat, cover the pan and simmer the soup for 30 minutes.

5 Stir in the crab meat and cook for 5 minutes, until heated through. Taste and adjust the seasoning, adding a little pepper sauce if desired. Serve immediately in warmed soup bowls.

Crab and Spinach Soup

Corn Chowder

Corn Chowder can be made with milk or chicken stock. Served with freshly made popcorn, this filling soup is almost a meal in itself.

1 tablespoon oil
175g/6oz bacon, diced
1 large Spanish onion, finely chopped
2 celery stalks, finely chopped
1 green pepper, seeded and diced
2 tomatoes, skinned, seeded and diced
2 potatoes, peeled and diced
300g/11oz can sweetcorn kernels
700ml/1¼ pints milk or chicken stock
1 teaspoon salt
freshly ground black pepper
dash of Tabasco

For the popcorn
2 tablespoons oil
50g/2oz popcorn kernels
salt

Serves 6

1 Heat the oil in a large saucepan, and fry the diced bacon over moderate heat for 5 minutes until crisp and brown.

2 Using a slotted spoon, transfer the bacon on to absorbent paper to drain.

3 Add the onion to the pan and fry for 5 minutes, until soft and golden. Stir in the celery, green pepper, tomatoes and potatoes and cook the vegetables for a further 3 minutes.

4 Add the sweetcorn and pour over the milk or stock. Season with salt, pepper and a dash of Tabasco. Bring gently to simmering point, then lower the heat and simmer for 15 minutes.

5 Meanwhile make the popcorn: heat the oil in a large saucepan and add the popcorn kernels. Cover the pan and, holding the lid on tightly, shake the pan from time to time as soon as the corn starts popping. When all the popping has stopped remove the lid and transfer the popcorn to a serving bowl. Sprinkle over salt to taste.

6 To serve, ladle the soup into warmed soup bowls and sprinkle over the crispy bacon. Hand the popcorn round separately.

Making Coconut Milk and Cream

To open a coconut: pierce the eyes of the coconut and drain out the liquid. Place the coconut on a cloth on a firm surface and split it open with a cleaver or hammer. Remove and grate the flesh. Remove the brown skin if the flesh is to be used in a recipe.
To make fresh coconut milk: blend the flesh and liquid of one fresh coconut with 225ml/8fl oz boiling water in an electric blender, then strain through a muslin-lined sieve, twisting the cloth to extract all the liquid from the flesh (makes approximately 350ml/12fl oz). For a less rich milk, mix the coconut flesh and water in the same way and set aside for 1 hour before straining as above. For a thinner milk, repeat the above process twice, using a further 225ml/8fl oz of water.

To make quick coconut milk: use desiccated coconut in the same way as fresh (500g/18oz desiccated coconut is equal to 3 fresh coconuts), substitute hot milk instead of water for a richer result. Packaged coconut cream can be mixed with water to make varying thicknesses of coconut milk. Canned coconut milk is available from health food shops and ethnic food stores.
To make coconut cream: make fresh coconut milk, using half the amount of water and set aside until the cream rises to the top.

Black-Eyed Bean and Coconut Soup

Black-eyed beans, also known as cowpeas, give this thick and spicy soup an interesting nutty flavour. Serve with crusty French bread and a cooling glass of white wine.

225g/8oz dried black-eyed beans
275g/10oz piece smoked gammon (preferably on the bone)
1 bay leaf
2 onions, chopped
2 whole cloves
1 teaspoon sugar
1 tablespoon oil
2 tomatoes, skinned and chopped
600ml/1 pint coconut milk (see below)
2 sprigs fresh thyme
1 teaspoon salt
freshly ground black pepper
1 hot seasoning pepper
50ml/2fl oz sherry or rum

Serves 6

1 Soak the beans in cold water overnight.

2 Drain and refresh under cold water. Put the beans in a large saucepan with the smoked gammon.

3 Pour in enough cold water to cover (about 1.1l/2 pints), add the bay leaf, half the onion, cloves and sugar and bring to the boil over moderate heat. Boil for 10 minutes, skimming off any scum that rises to the surface. Lower the heat, cover the pan and simmer for 45 minutes, or until the beans are cooked and the meat is tender. Remove from the heat and strain the stock into a bowl. Add the beans to the strained stock.

4 Trim the meat from the gammon bone, discarding any skin or fat and cut into small dice. Set aside.

5 Heat the oil in a saucepan and fry the remaining onion for 5 minutes over moderate heat, stirring constantly, until soft and golden. Add the tomatoes and cook for 3 minutes, stirring constantly.

6 Pour over the coconut milk and add the reserved beans and stock. Season with thyme, salt, freshly ground black pepper and the seasoning pepper and bring to the boil. Lower the heat, cover and cook for 5 minutes.

7 Remove from the heat and discard the seasoning pepper. Allow to cool slightly before liquidizing in a food processor or blender.

8 Pour the soup into a clean saucepan. Add the reserved gammon and sherry or rum and cook gently over low heat for 5 minutes until heated through.

9 Taste and adjust seasoning. Ladle into warmed soup bowls and serve immediately.

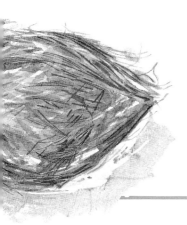

Pumpkin Soup

Pumpkin Soup is packed full of vitamins, using the cooking liquid as stock. Pale orange in colour, it is found throughout the Caribbean and is often known as Sunshine Soup.

1kg/2lb 3 oz pumpkin, peeled, deseeded and cut into 2.5cm/1in cubes
salt and freshly ground black pepper
2 tablespoons butter
1 large onion, finely chopped
3 spring onions, trimmed and finely chopped
3 tomatoes, skinned and chopped
225ml/8fl oz coconut milk (see page 16)
¼ teaspoon grated nutmeg
pinch of cayenne pepper
150ml/¼ pint soured cream

Serves 4-6

1 Put the pumpkin into a saucepan, add enough water to cover (about 900ml/1½ pints) and 1 teaspoon of salt. Bring to the boil. Lower the heat and simmer for 20 minutes. Drain, and reserve the cooking liquid.

2 Melt the butter in a saucepan over moderate heat. Add the onion and spring onions and fry, stirring constantly, for 5 minutes until soft and golden.

3 Add the pumpkin, tomatoes, coconut milk, 700ml/1¼ pints of the pumpkin cooking liquid, ⅛ teaspoon of the nutmeg, a pinch of cayenne pepper and salt and black pepper to taste. Bring to the boil, lower the heat, cover and simmer for 30 minutes.

4 Remove the pan from the heat, allow to cool slightly, then liquidize half the soup at a time in a food processor or blender. Return to the pan and heat for 5 minutes until warmed through.

5 Pour the soup into a warmed tureen and swirl the soured cream on top. Sprinkle with the remaining nutmeg and serve the soup at once.

Tomato and Sweet Potato Soup

Sweet potatoes are one of the more interesting of the Caribbean starchy vegetables. Their slight sweetness combined with tomatoes is unusual but delicious.

1 tablespoon oil
1 tablespoon butter
2 onions, finely chopped
225g/8oz sweet potatoes, peeled and diced
450g/1lb tomatoes, skinned and finely chopped
juice and grated rind of 1 large orange
900ml/1½ pints chicken stock
1 teaspoon oregano
1 teaspoon salt
freshly ground black pepper

To garnish
1 orange, thinly sliced
1 tomato, thinly sliced

Serves 6

1 Heat the oil and butter together in a saucepan over moderate heat. Add the onions and cook for 5 minutes, or until soft and golden.

2 Add the sweet potatoes, tomatoes, orange juice and rind, chicken stock, oregano, salt and pepper and bring to the boil. Lower the heat, cover the pan and simmer the soup for 20 minutes.

3 Remove the pan from the heat and allow to cool slightly. Liquidize half the soup at a time in a blender or food processor.

4 Return to the pan and heat for 5 minutes until warmed through.

5 To serve, ladle into warmed soup bowls and garnish with a slice of orange and a slice of tomato.

Pumpkin Soup

Fish and Coconut Soup
Sopito

Fish and Coconut Soup is better known as Sopito in the Dutch islands of Curaçao and Aruba. The tasty combination of coconut milk, fish, salt meat, hot seasoning pepper and spices gives this delicious soup its unusual flavour. It is sometimes made with cream, making it a much richer dish.

2 onions
1 garlic clove
2 bay leaves
1 celery stalk, chopped
1 leek, chopped
1 teaspoon whole peppercorns
1 tablespoon finely chopped fresh basil
1 teaspoon cumin seeds
salt
450g/1lb whole fish, sea bream, red snapper, sea bass or mullet, cleaned and scaled
100g/4oz salt beef, diced
2 whole cloves
1 hot seasoning pepper
300ml/½ pint coconut milk, made with fresh coconut (see page 16)
3 tablespoons cornmeal
225g/8oz unshelled prawns
1 tablespoon finely chopped fresh basil, to garnish

Serves 6

1 Slice one of the onions and put it into a saucepan with the garlic, bay leaves, celery, leek, peppercorns, 1 tablespoon basil, cumin and 1 teaspoon of salt. Pour over 1.1l/2 pints cold water and bring to the boil over moderate heat. Lower the heat, cover the pan and simmer for 15 minutes.

2 Add the fish and cook for 10-15 minutes, until the fish flakes easily when tested with a fork.

3 Remove the pan from the heat and strain the stock into a clean pan. Reserve the fish.

4 Finely chop the remaining onion and add this to the fish stock together with the diced beef, cloves, seasoning pepper and coconut milk.

5 Bring to the boil over moderate heat. Lower the heat, cover and simmer for 45 minutes, or until the beef is tender. Remove the seasoning pepper after 15 minutes and discard.

6 Sprinkle over the cornmeal and cook for 2 minutes, stirring constantly.

7 Skin and bone the fish and cut it into 2.5cm/1in pieces. Add the fish and prawns to the soup and cook over low heat for 5 minutes to heat through.

8 To serve, ladle into warmed soup bowls and sprinkle over the chopped basil to garnish.

Pepper Pot Soup

A filling and spicy soup made with vegetables, meat and prawns which is found on several of the Caribbean islands. It is often confused with another well-known Caribbean dish called 'Pepperpot' made from mixed meat, seasonings and cassareep. Like Pepperpot, this soup improves with age, so make it the day before it is to be served.

450g/1lb shin of beef, cut into 1.5cm/½in cubes
225g/8oz salt beef, cut into 1.5cm/½in cubes
450g/1lb fresh spinach, trimmed
salt and freshly ground black pepper
2 onions, finely chopped
2 garlic cloves, crushed
1 teaspoon dried thyme
1 hot seasoning pepper
450g/1lb tannias, peeled and cut into 2.5cm/1in cubes
225g/8oz unshelled prawns
1.1l/2 pints beef stock
2 tablespoons butter
100g/4oz okra, trimmed and finely sliced

Serves 6-8

1 Put the beef and salt beef into a large saucepan. Pour over enough cold water to cover (about 2.3l/4 pints) and bring to the boil. Lower the heat and simmer for 1½ hours.

2 Put the spinach in another pan and cover with cold water. Add 1 teaspoon of salt and bring to the boil over moderate heat. Cook for 10 minutes, then drain. Transfer to a food processor or blender and process for 30 seconds until the spinach forms a smooth purée.

3 Add the spinach purée to the meat in the saucepan, together with the onions, garlic, thyme, seasoning pepper, tannias and prawns, and season to taste with salt and black pepper. Pour over the stock and bring to the boil over moderate heat. Lower the heat and simmer for 20 minutes, or until the meat and tannias are tender.

4 Melt the butter in a small frying-pan, add the okra and fry over moderate heat, stirring constantly for 5 minutes or until lightly browned. Add to the soup and cook for 5 minutes.

5 Remove the seasoning pepper, transfer to a warmed soup tureen and serve immediately.

Chicken Consommé with Peppers

This delicate consommé, flavoured with sweet peppers and a dash of sherry or Pepper Wine (see page 95), makes an ideal beginning to a Caribbean meal.

2 spring onions, trimmed and finely sliced
1 green pepper, seeded and finely sliced
1 red pepper, seeded and finely sliced
dry sherry or Pepper Wine (see page 95), to serve

For the stock
1.6kg/3½lb chicken
1 large onion, chopped
2 carrots, chopped
1 celery stalk, chopped
½ red pepper, seeded and chopped
1 tomato, chopped
1 small turnip, chopped
1 teaspoon salt
1 teaspoon sugar
1 teaspoon whole black peppercorns

Serves 8

1 First make the stock: wash the chicken then place it in a large saucepan. Add the onion, carrots, celery, red pepper, tomato, turnip, salt, sugar and peppercorns. Pour over enough cold water to cover (about 2.8l/5 pints) and bring to the boil over moderate heat. Boil for 10 minutes, skimming off any scum that rises to the surface.

2 Lower the heat, cover the pan and simmer for 3 hours. Drain the stock into a bowl and leave until cool, then cover the bowl with cling film and refrigerate overnight.

3 Remove the fat from the surface of the stock, then strain the stock into a saucepan.

4 Heat the stock until just simmering, then add the spring onions, green and red peppers. Cook the soup for 4 minutes.

5 To serve, ladle into warmed soup bowls and add a dash of sherry or pepper wine to each bowl.

STARTERS AND SNACKS

My favourite dishes in the Caribbean have always been the Starters and Snacks. Many of the dishes in the snack section are eaten as light meals by themselves at varying times of the day. For example Salt Cod Salad (Buljol, see page 24) and Cornmeal and Meat Parcels (Pastelles, see page 30) can be eaten for breakfast, lunch or supper.

Fish Mousse

This delicate creamy Fish Mousse from Martinique makes an impressive first course for a dinner party. Serve the mousse with hot Melba toast and a bottle of cold Chablis.

In Martinique red snapper would be used for this dish, but any firm-fleshed white fish can be used as a substitute.

1 teaspoon oil
350g/12oz white fish fillets, snapper, haddock or red fish
1 onion, sliced
1 bay leaf
6 whole peppercorns
1 teaspoon salt
225g/8oz cream cheese, softened
6 tablespoons mayonnaise
1 tablespoon finely grated onion
100g/4oz shelled prawns, chopped
1 tablespoon finely chopped fresh parsley
1 tablespoon finely chopped fresh chives
1/8 teaspoon cayenne pepper
pinch of grated nutmeg
juice of 2 limes
1 tablespoon powdered gelatine

To garnish
1 bunch watercress, trimmed
1 lime, sliced

Serves 8

1 Using the teaspoon of oil lightly grease a 750ml/26fl oz fish-shaped or plain mould.

2 Place the fish in a saucepan and cover with cold water. Add the sliced onion, bay leaf, peppercorns and salt. Bring to the boil over moderate heat. Lower the heat, cover the pan and simmer for 10 minutes, or until the fish flakes easily with a fork.

3 Drain the fish, remove any bones and discard the seasonings. Put the fish in a food processor with the cream cheese, mayonnaise and grated onion and process for 30 seconds to form a smooth purée.

4 Add the prawns, parsley, chives, cayenne pepper and nutmeg and process for 15 seconds.

5 Sprinkle the gelatine over the lime juice in a heatproof bowl. Leave to soak for 5 minutes, then stand the bowl in a pan of gently simmering water for 1-2 minutes until the gelatine has completely dissolved, stirring occasionally. Pour the gelatine into the fish mixture. Process for 10 seconds until thoroughly combined. Pour the mixture into the prepared mould, cover with cling film and refrigerate for 2 hours or until set.

6 To serve, line a serving platter with watercress, then dip the bottom of the mould into hot water for a few seconds. Run a knife around inside edge of mould then turn out mousse on to the platter, giving a few firm shakes. Decorate with lime slices.

Fish Mousse (left) and Salt Cod Salad

Marinated Cooked Fish
Escovitch

Escovitch comes from the Spanish word 'escabeche', which is a popular cooking method of pickling cooked fish in vinegar.

1kg/2lb 3oz fish fillets, cod, red snapper,
mackerel, red mullet or salmon
juice of 2 limes
1 onion, finely chopped
1 garlic clove, crushed
1 teaspoon salt
freshly ground black pepper
6 tablespoons olive oil

For the sauce
2 tablespoons oil
2 onions, finely sliced
2 garlic cloves, crushed
1 red pepper, seeded and finely sliced
1 green pepper, seeded and finely sliced
2.5cm/1in piece of fresh root ginger,
peeled and finely chopped
pinch of ground mace
1 tablespoon black peppercorns
2 bay leaves
1 teaspoon salt
175ml/6fl oz white wine vinegar

Serves 4-6

1 Season the fish with the lime juice, onion, garlic, salt and pepper, cover and marinate for 2 hours.

2 Make the sauce: heat the oil in a saucepan, add the onions and fry gently over moderate heat for 5 minutes, stirring constantly. Add the garlic, red and green peppers and cook for 3 minutes.

3 Add the remaining ingredients with 125ml/4fl oz water. Bring to the boil, then lower the heat and simmer for 10 minutes. Remove from the heat.

4 Drain the fish and discard the seasonings. Pat dry with absorbent paper. Heat half the oil in a frying-pan and fry half the fish for 6-8 minutes, or until lightly browned, turning once. Transfer to a shallow serving dish. Repeat with remaining oil and fish.

5 Pour sauce over fish and serve hot or cold.

Salt Cod Salad
Buljol

This spicy salad is a great favourite for Sunday breakfast in Trinidad. It is also delicious as an appetizer served on little crackers, to eat with drinks.
 This dish should be made the day before you wish to eat it.

225g/8oz salt cod, soaked overnight and drained
juice of 1 lime
1 large Spanish onion, finely chopped
1 green pepper, seeded and finely chopped
3 tomatoes, chopped
3-4 tablespoons olive oil
2 hard-boiled eggs, finely chopped
2 tablespoons finely chopped fresh parsley
freshly ground black pepper

Serves 6

1 Put the fish in a saucepan, cover with cold water and bring to the boil over moderate heat. Lower the heat and simmer for 1 minute. Remove from the heat, drain and refresh under cold water.

2 When just cool enough to handle, remove and discard the skin and bones and shred the fish. Place the shredded fish in a serving bowl.

3 Add the lime juice, onion, green pepper and tomatoes to the warm fish and mix well together.

4 Add 3 tablespoons of the oil and if the salad is a little dry, add the remaining oil. It should be lightly coated with the oil.

5 Stir in the eggs and parsley and black pepper to taste. When completely cool, cover with cling film and refrigerate for at least 4 hours or overnight. Remove from the refrigerator 1 hour before serving.

Trinidad Fried Shark

One of the many treats of spending a hot Sunday at Maraccas Beach is having an ice cold beer or two with your tasty beach snack of Shark and Bake.

This fearsome animal tastes quite delicious when highly seasoned and fried, then served in the bun-like Bake (see page 117). The brave eat it with generous helpings of Hot Pepper Sauce (see page 95), followed by more cool beer to put out the fire. The texture of shark is often compared to that of veal.

1 kg/2lb 3oz shark, skinned and cut into 5cm/2in cubes
4 tablespoons flour
1 teaspoon dried thyme
1 teaspoon salt
freshly ground black pepper
oil, for deep-frying

For the marinade
juice of 2 limes
1 onion, finely chopped
2 garlic cloves, crushed
1 fresh chilli, seeded and finely chopped
1 tablespoon dried thyme
1 teaspoon salt

Serves 4-6

1 Make the marinade: mix the lime juice, onion, garlic, chilli, thyme, salt and pepper together.

2 Place the shark cubes in a large mixing bowl, pour on the marinade and mix well.

3 Cover and place in the refrigerator for at least 2 hours or overnight.

4 Remove the shark from the marinade and pat dry with absorbent paper.

5 Season the flour with the thyme, salt and pepper and sprinkle on to a plate. Roll the shark in the flour.

6 Heat about 5cm/2in of oil in a deep frying-pan over moderate heat. When hot, add a few shark cubes at a time and fry for 5-7 minutes, until the fish is cooked through when tested with a knife. Remove with a slotted spoon and drain on absorbent paper. Keep warm in a low oven while frying the remaining shark.

Salt Cod Fritters
Stamp and Go

Salt Cod Fritters are to be found throughout the Caribbean, with each island having its own variation.

This recipe is for the Jamaican Stamp and Go – a name which apparently comes from an old nautical term. There are many other local names in the other islands for these fritters, Bacalaitos, Acrat de Morue or Marinades, John Staggerback or Poor Man's Fritters, to name but a few.

225g/8oz salt cod
100g/4oz flour
1 teaspoon baking powder
1/2 teaspoon salt
1 egg, lightly beaten
175ml/6fl oz milk
1 tablespoon melted butter
1 onion, finely grated
1 fresh red chilli, seeded and finely chopped
oil, for deep-frying

Makes 24

1 Soak the salt cod in water overnight. Drain, rinse under cold water, then place in a saucepan and cover with cold water.

2 Place the pan over moderate heat and bring to the boil. Reduce the heat, cover the pan and simmer for 10 minutes. Drain, rinse under cold water and, when cool enough to handle, remove and discard the skin and bones and flake the fish. Set aside.

3 Mix the flour, baking powder and salt together in a bowl. Make a well in the centre and pour in the egg, milk and melted butter. Mix together with a wooden spoon to make a smooth batter. Stir in the onion, chilli and flaked fish and mix well.

4 Heat about 1.5cm/1/2in of oil in a large deep frying-pan until hot but not smoking. Drop tablespoons of the mixture into the oil, a few at a time, spaced well apart. Fry for 3-4 minutes, turning once, or until golden brown.

5 Remove with a slotted spoon and drain on absorbent paper. Keep warm in a low oven while frying the remaining fritters. Serve hot.

Palm Heart Salad

A sophisticated starter from Martinique, this salad is served on individual plates, arranged in the shape of a palm tree. Palm hearts come from a wide variety of palms. The heart, which is the terminal bud of the palm, is edible and has a firm texture with a rather mild flavour.

Fresh palm hearts are generally boiled until tender then served either hot with a sauce as a vegetable dish, or cold in a salad.

400g/14oz can palm hearts, drained
2 firm ripe avocado pears
2 firm ripe mangoes, peeled and thinly sliced
juice of ½ lime
¼ Iceberg lettuce, thinly shredded

For the dressing
1 teaspoon mustard powder
1 teaspoon sugar
1 tablespoon mango chutney
2 tablespoons fresh lime juice
6 tablespoons olive oil
salt and freshly ground black pepper

Serves 6

1 Make the dressing: mix the mustard and sugar together in a mixing bowl. Add the chutney and lime juice then, using a balloon whisk, gradually whisk in the olive oil. Season with salt and pepper to taste, and strain through a sieve into a bowl, to remove any large pieces of mango.

2 Cut 6 large palm hearts into approximately 2.5cm/1in slices and re-form them individually on serving plates to represent palm 'trunks'. Chop the remaining smaller palm hearts into thinner slices – these will be the 'coconuts' – and set aside.

3 Peel and thinly slice the avocados. Arrange alternate slices of mango and avocado at the top of each palm heart 'trunk' to make the palm 'leaves' and add the remaining sliced palm hearts for the 'coconuts'. Pour the lime juice over the avocado slices to prevent them from discolouring.

4 Sprinkle a little shredded lettuce along the bottom of each plate for the 'grass' and serve with the dressing handed separately.

Shrimp and Watermelon Cocktail

Spicy, sweet and cool, this Shrimp and Watermelon Cocktail characterizes the balance of flavours in West Indian cooking.

The shellfish known as shrimps in the Caribbean are called prawns here. Serve this impressive starter in tall glasses with slices of brown bread and butter.

450g/1lb watermelon
350g/12oz shelled prawns
1 tablespoon fresh lime juice
1 tablespoon gin
¼ lettuce, finely shredded
1 lime, sliced, to garnish

For the dressing
3 tablespoons mayonnaise
3 tablespoons tomato ketchup
1 teaspoon Worcestershire sauce
1 tablespoon finely grated onion
1 teaspoon paprika
½ teaspoon salt
½ teaspoon white pepper
dash of Tabasco

Serves 6

1 Remove the seeds from the watermelon and scoop the flesh into balls using a melon baller.

2 Reserve 18 prawns and 18 melon balls to use for the garnish.

3 Put the remaining prawns in a bowl and pour over the lime juice and gin. Set aside.

4 Make the dressing: mix the mayonnaise, ketchup, Worcestershire sauce, onion, paprika, salt, pepper and Tabasco together in a large mixing bowl.

5 Tip the prawns with their liquid into the dressing and add the melon balls. Mix well to ensure the prawns and melon are coated with the dressing.

6 Put the shredded lettuce into the bottom of 6 tall glasses. Spoon the prawn and melon mixture into the glasses. Garnish with the reserved melon balls and prawns and the lime slices and serve immediately.

Palm Heart Salad

Hot Orange and Grapefruit Baskets

A great way to start any Caribbean meal – juicy citrus fruits with a good shot of rum.

These attractive grapefruit baskets are filled with a mixture of grapefruit and orange segments that have been tossed in rum, then sprinkled with Demerara sugar and baked under the grill until the sugar is bubbling up. Many other citrus fruits may be used for this recipe including limes, tangerines, tangelos, uglis and shaddocks.

2 grapefruits
4 oranges
2-3 tablespoons rum
4 tablespoons Demerara sugar
dash of Angostura bitters

Serves 4

1 Using a small, sharp knife, cut each grapefruit in half using a zig-zag line. Pull the fruit apart and cut the flesh from inside with a grapefruit knife, removing all the pith and leaving a clean grapefruit skin basket. Cut a paper-thin slice from the bottom of each basket to enable it to stand firmly.

2 Cut the pith away from the grapefruit segments and cut the flesh up into chunks. Place the segments in a mixing bowl.

3 Peel and segment each orange in the following way: using a very sharp knife cut off the two ends of the orange. Stand the orange on one end and cut off the skin in a downwards motion, taking the pith with the skin. Cut each orange segment from between the pithy membranes. Add the orange segments to the grapefruit chunks. Pour over the rum and mix well together.

4 Spoon the mixture into the grapefruit baskets, decorating the top of each basket with 3 of the orange segments.

5 Heat the grill to high.

6 Sprinkle a tablespoon of the sugar over each grapefruit. Place the grapefruits in a grill pan and grill for 5 minutes, until the fruit is heated through and the sugar is bubbling.

7 Arrange on individual plates, add a dash of Angostura bitters to each portion and serve the grapefruit baskets immediately.

Plantain Crisps

Plantain Crisps are crunchy, with a mild banana flavour. They can be kept for several weeks in a screw-top jar and eaten as a snack on their own or as the perfect accompaniment to a dip. Plantain Crisps are a must at any West Indian cocktail party.

4 green plantains
oil, for deep-frying
salt

1 Peel the plantains and cut into thin slices.

2 Heat the oil in a deep frying-pan.

3 When the oil is hot, add the plantain slices, a few at a time, and fry for 2-3 minutes until crisp and golden. Remove them with a slotted spoon and drain on absorbent paper.

4 Sprinkle over the salt to taste. Serve when cool.

Soused Pigs Trotters
Souse

Soused Pigs Trotters, or Souse as it is also called, is traditionally served together with black pudding for an informal Sunday brunch. It is often made with 'hog features' – pig's head. For a more meaty dish, pork chops may also be added.

4 meaty pigs trotters

For the brine
juice of 12 limes
1-2 tablespoons salt
2 onions, chopped
2 fresh chillies, seeded and finely chopped

To garnish
1 cucumber, peeled and sliced
watercress sprigs

Serves 4

1 Put the pigs trotters in a metal colander, then pour over boiling water to scald them. Rinse under cold water and scrape clean with a knife.

2 Put the trotters into a large saucepan, cover with cold water, then bring to the boil over moderate heat. Lower the heat, cover the pan and simmer the trotters for 1½ hours until tender.

3 Drain the trotters, then refresh under cold water. When just cool enough to handle, split down the middle, then cut into bite-size pieces and place in a large bowl.

4 Make the brine: mix the limes, salt, onions and chillies together in a bowl, then pour over the warm pigs trotters. Add enough cold water to cover the trotters. Cover the bowl with cling film and refrigerate overnight.

5 To serve, remove trotters from the brine and arrange in a serving dish. Garnish with the cucumber slices and watercress.

Cornmeal and Meat Parcels
Pastelles

Originally from South America, these banana leaf parcels of cornmeal and meat are a national favourite in Trinidad. They make a perfect snack at any time of the day, and are even eaten for breakfast with Hot Pepper Sauce (see page 95).

Making pastelles can be a great way to spend an afternoon, with a group of family or friends forming a production line – one person preparing the banana leaves, another rolling the cornmeal balls, another adding the meat and yet another folding the parcels. They are generally made in great quantities just before Christmas but are also eaten throughout the year.

450g/1lb coarse cornmeal
25g/1oz margarine, cut into cubes
5 tablespoons oil
2 teaspoons salt
3-4 banana leaves

For the filling
2 tablespoons oil
1 large onion, finely chopped
1 garlic clove, crushed
1 fresh chilli, seeded and finely chopped
225g/8oz stewing pork, minced or finely chopped
225g/8oz stewing beef, minced or finely chopped
1 teaspoon finely chopped fresh thyme
1 tablespoon finely chopped fresh chives
1 teaspoon finely chopped fresh basil
2 tomatoes, skinned and chopped
½ red pepper, seeded and finely chopped
1 tablespoon Worcestershire sauce
4 tablespoons capers, chopped
4 tablespoons raisins
15 olives, chopped
salt and freshly ground black pepper
175ml/6fl oz beef stock

Makes 18

1 Make the filling: heat the oil in a frying-pan and fry the onion gently for 5 minutes, or until soft. Stir in the garlic and chilli and cook for 3 minutes.

2 Add the pork, beef, thyme, chives and basil and cook for 10-15 minutes, stirring constantly, until the meat is lightly browned.

3 Stir in the tomatoes, red pepper, Worcestershire sauce, half the capers, raisins and olives and season. Pour over the stock and bring to the boil. Lower heat and simmer, uncovered, for 45 minutes, stirring occasionally. Adjust seasoning, then set aside to cool.

4 Put the cornmeal into a large mixing bowl, add the margarine, 2 tablespoons oil and the salt. Pour over 650ml/22fl oz boiling water and mix well with a metal spatula to form a smooth dough. Form the cornmeal into 18 balls.

5 Cut the banana leaves into thirty-six 20 × 25cm/ 8 × 10in rectangles. Place in a bowl, then pour over boiling water. Drain, then refresh under cold water. Pat dry with absorbent paper.

6 Rub a leaf with a little of the remaining oil. Place a ball of cornmeal in the centre and gently pat down to form a circle about 5mm/¼in thick. Spread 2 tablespoons of the filling over the cornmeal and sprinkle over a little of the remaining capers, raisins and olives.

7 Enclose the meat filling with cornmeal by folding half the leaf over, bringing the cornmeal with it. Flatten leaf, then repeat with other half of leaf so that the cornmeal completely encloses the meat. Then fold up the leaf to make a parcel. Place the parcel folded side down on another leaf, on the opposite grain, and fold to enclose the parcel, securing with string. Foil may be used instead of the second leaf, with the ends tightly folded.

8 Repeat, to make 17 more pastelles. Place in a pan of boiling salted water and simmer for 1½ hours.

9 Drain the pastelles well, then remove the string or foil. Transfer to a large platter and serve.

Cornmeal and Meat Parcels

Salt Fish and Ackee

One of the most popular dishes of Jamaica, this can be served as a starter or as a main course, with fried plantain and Rice 'n' Peas (see page 80).

Ackees are the fruit of a West African tree (*Blighia sapida*), generally believed to have been named after Captain Bligh. The tree has pear-shaped pods which, when ripe, split open bearing three shiny black seeds each surrounded by a cream-coloured aril, which is the edible part. The aril has a delicate flavour and is often compared to 'brains' in appearance when uncooked and 'scrambled eggs' when cooked. The fruit must be eaten only when just ripe, as both unripe and overripe ackee can be very poisonous.

225g/8oz salt cod
25g/1oz butter
50ml/2fl oz olive oil
2 rashers streaky bacon, diced
4 spring onions, trimmed and finely chopped
1 onion, finely sliced
½ teaspoon dried thyme
2 fresh chillies, seeded and finely sliced
1 green pepper, seeded and finely sliced
2 tomatoes, skinned and chopped
350g/12oz can ackees, drained
salt and freshly ground black pepper
parsley sprigs, to garnish

Serves 4-6

1 Put the fish in a saucepan and cover with water. Bring to the boil and cook for 10 minutes. Drain the fish, then rinse under cold water. When cool enough to handle, remove and discard the skin and bones and flake the fish. Set aside.

2 Heat the butter with the oil in a frying-pan over moderate heat. Add the bacon and fry for 5 minutes until quite crispy. Remove with a slotted spoon and drain on absorbent paper.

3 Fry the spring onions, onion, thyme, chillies and green pepper together in the pan for 5 minutes. Add the tomatoes and cook for a further 5 minutes.

4 Stir in the salt cod, ackees and bacon and cook for 2-3 minutes, until heated. Transfer to a serving dish, garnish with the parsley and serve immediately.

Avocado Dip

This hot and spicy dip is a delicious appetizer to hand around with drinks. Serve with Plantain Crisps (see page 29) or crudités.

2 ripe avocado pears
1 tablespoon fresh lime juice
1 garlic clove, crushed
1 tablespoon finely grated onion
175g/6oz cream cheese, softened
3 tablespoons coconut milk (see page 16)
⅛ teaspoon ground pimento
dash of Tabasco
1 teaspoon ground coriander
salt and freshly ground black pepper
fresh coriander leaves or parsley, to garnish

Serves 6-8

1 Peel the avocados and mash the pulp with a fork or blend in a food processor until smooth and creamy. Add the lime juice, garlic and onion.

2 Stir in the cream cheese, coconut milk, pimento, Tabasco and ground coriander. Mix well and season to taste with salt and pepper.

3 Spoon the dip into a serving dish, garnish with the coriander leaves or parsley and serve immediately. If you wish to make the dip a few hours before serving, keep one of the avocado stones and immerse it in the dip. Cover with cling film and refrigerate. This will prevent the avocado from discolouring unattractively.

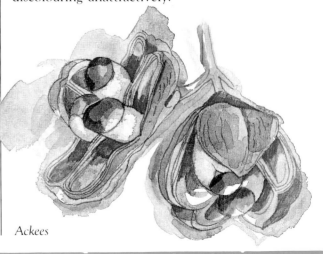

Ackees

Jamaican Beef Patties

One of the most popular lunchtime snacks in Jamaica, these patties are a great alternative to the American hamburger or the English sandwich.

They were brought to Jamaica from Haiti with the immigrants who settled there in the 18th century. They are best eaten freshly baked as they tend to dry out if kept for any length of time. Commercially prepared curry powder may be used as an alternative to the different spices used to flavour the meat.

For the pastry
450g/1lb plain flour
2 teaspoons turmeric
1 teaspoon salt
225g/8oz margarine, cut into cubes

For the filling
2 tablespoons oil
1 onion, finely chopped
2 spring onions, trimmed and finely chopped
1-2 garlic cloves, crushed
2 fresh chillies, seeded and finely chopped
350g/12oz minced beef
4 tomatoes, skinned and chopped
1/4 teaspoon turmeric
1/4 teaspoon ground cumin
1/4 teaspoon ground coriander
1/4 teaspoon ground fenugreek
1/4 teaspoon ground ginger
1/8 teaspoon ground cinnamon
1/8 teaspoon ground cardamom
salt and freshly ground black pepper
2 egg yolks, beaten

Makes 12

1 Make the pastry: sift the flour, turmeric and salt into a bowl. Add the margarine and mix together until the mixture resembles coarse breadcrumbs. Add 3 tablespoons of iced water to form a firm dough. Cover the dough with cling film and refrigerate for 2 hours or longer.

2 Meanwhile, prepare the filling: heat the oil in a frying-pan, add the onion and fry over moderate heat for 5 minutes, until soft and golden. Stir in the spring onions, garlic and chillies and cook for 3 minutes.

3 Add the beef and fry, stirring frequently, for 10 minutes. Stir in the tomatoes, turmeric, cumin, coriander, fenugreek, ginger, cinnamon and cardamom and season to taste with salt and freshly ground pepper.

4 Pour in 125ml/4fl oz water, reduce the heat to low and cook for 20 minutes, stirring frequently. Set aside to cool.

5 Heat the oven to 200C/400F/Gas 6.

6 Roll out the pastry and cut into 12 circles, approximately 18cm/7in in diameter, using a saucer as a template.

7 Put 2 tablespoons of the filling on one side of the pastry circle then fold over to form a crescent. Crimp the edges with a fork to seal them. Arrange on an ungreased baking sheet and brush the top of each patty with a little beaten egg yolk.

8 Bake in the centre of the oven for 25-30 minutes until golden brown.

9 Transfer to a large serving platter and serve the beef patties at once.

FISH DISHES

One of the most delightful experiences in the Caribbean is to get up early in the morning to meet the local fishing boats and choose your fish for the day. The choice is quite dazzling: silver-winged flying fish, rosy red snappers, lobsters, shrimps and many many more. Although the Caribbean waters abound with fresh fish, salt cod is still used a great deal. Dating from the days of slavery, its distinctive flavour is essential to many traditional dishes.

Poached Fish with Avocado Sauce

This elegant dish can be served either hot or cold. Garnish the fish with the avocado slices just before serving to avoid the possibility of discoloration.

1 onion, sliced
1 celery stalk, sliced
1 carrot, sliced
1 lime, sliced
½ teaspoon whole black peppercorns
1 bay leaf
1 tablespoon finely chopped fresh parsley
1 sprig fresh thyme
300ml/½ pint dry white wine
2 whole fish, each weighing 1.4kg/3lb, bream, bass or red snapper, cleaned

For the sauce
2 firm ripe avocado pears
2 tablespoons lime juice
2 tablespoons olive oil
1 tablespoon grated onion
2 garlic cloves, crushed
¼ teaspoon dried oregano
1 teaspoon salt
freshly ground black pepper

To garnish
2 stuffed olives, sliced
2 small firm ripe avocado pears
1 tablespoon fresh lime juice
fresh coriander leaves

Serves 8

1 Put the onion, celery, carrot, lime, peppercorns, bay leaf, parsley, thyme and wine into a fish kettle. Pour over 2.3l/4 pints of water and bring to the boil. Lower the heat, cover with the lid and simmer for 20 minutes.

2 Place the fish on the poaching tray and gently lower them into the liquid. If necessary add a little more water to cover the fish and bring back to the boil. Lower the heat, cover and simmer for 5 minutes. Turn off the heat and leave the fish for 1 hour to cool in the liquid.

3 Lift out the tray and carefully skin one side of each fish, leaving the skin on the head. Carefully turn each fish on to a serving platter, skinned side down, and skin the other half.

4 Make the sauce: peel and chop the avocados. Put them with the lime juice, olive oil, onion, garlic, oregano, salt and pepper into a food processor or blender and process for 30 seconds or until they form a smooth purée.

5 Spread the avocado purée over the skinned part of the fish, but not the heads and tails. Cover each eye with olive slices. Peel, quarter and thinly slice the avocados. Put them in a bowl, pour over the lime juice and mix gently. Garnish the fish with the sliced avocado to form 'scales', decorate with coriander leaves and serve immediately.

Poached Fish with Avocado Sauce

Frizzled Salt Cod

This is a rather exotic way of serving scrambled eggs. Salt cod can be bought from many delicatessens either in a whole piece or filleted and then wrapped in plastic.

225g/8oz salt cod, soaked overnight and drained
3 rashers bacon, finely chopped
100g/4oz fresh spinach, washed, dried and
finely chopped
2 tablespoons butter
2 tablespoons oil
1 onion, finely chopped
3 spring onions, trimmed and finely chopped
2 tomatoes, finely chopped
½ red pepper, seeded and finely chopped
½ teaspoon dried basil
salt and freshly ground black pepper
2 eggs, beaten
1 tablespoon finely chopped fresh chives, to garnish

Serves 4

1 Put the salt cod in a saucepan. Pour over enough cold water to cover and bring to the boil over moderate heat. Lower the heat and simmer for 5 minutes. Drain and refresh under cold water. When cool enough to handle, remove and discard the skin and bones.

2 Put the fish in a blender or food processor and process for 30 seconds. Transfer to a bowl.

3 Add the bacon and spinach to the salt cod and mix well together.

4 Melt the butter and the oil together in a heavy-based frying-pan over moderate heat. Add the onion and fry, stirring constantly for 5 minutes, until soft and golden.

5 Stir in the fish mixture, spring onions, tomatoes, red pepper and basil. Add salt and pepper to taste and cook over moderate to high heat, for 5 minutes, stirring frequently.

6 Pour over the beaten eggs and cook, stirring constantly for 2 minutes, until the eggs are cooked.

7 Transfer to a warmed serving dish, sprinkle over the chives and serve immediately.

Fish with Coriander and Coconut

Fish with Coriander and Coconut reflects the South American influence on the cooking of the Caribbean. Serve with Creole Rice (see page 81) and Avocado and Pink Grapefruit Salad (see page 90). Coriander, also known as cilantro, was brought originally from southern Europe.

700g/1½lb cod fillets, skinned
juice of 1 lime
salt and freshly ground black pepper
2 Spanish onions, thinly sliced
2 tablespoons olive oil
4 spring onions, trimmed and chopped
2 garlic cloves, crushed
1 fresh chilli, seeded and finely chopped
400g/14oz can tomatoes, drained and chopped
3 tablespoons finely chopped fresh parsley
5 tablespoons finely chopped fresh coriander
600ml/1 pint coconut milk (see page 16)
coriander sprigs, to garnish

Serves 6

1 Put the fish fillets in a glass or china dish. Pour over the lime juice. Add 1 teaspoon of salt and half the sliced onions. Mix the ingredients together and set aside for 30 minutes.

2 Heat the oil in a large heavy-based frying-pan, add the remaining onion and fry for 5 minutes over moderate heat. Add the spring onions, garlic and chilli and cook for 2 minutes, stirring constantly.

3 Add the tomatoes and cook for a further 5 minutes.

4 Lay the fish fillets in the pan and spoon over the tomato sauce. Sprinkle over the parsley and coriander. Season to taste with salt and black pepper. Pour over the coconut milk, and bring to the boil. Lower heat, cover pan and simmer for 15 minutes.

5 Taste and adjust the seasoning. Transfer to a warmed serving platter and garnish with coriander sprigs. Serve immediately.

Martinique Poached Fish
Court Bouillon de Poisson

Martinique Poached Fish is an adaptation of one of the most characteristic dishes of the French islands, Court Bouillon de Poisson. The term 'court bouillon' does not refer to the cooking liquid used for poaching, as in French cooking, but in this case is used to mean a fish cooked in a special sauce. In Martinique or Guadaloupe Court Bouillon de Poisson would be finished with the addition of raw garlic and lime juice. Serve with Creole Rice (see page 81), fried ripe plantain and Baked Christophenes au Gratin (see page 73).

1kg/2lb 3oz whole fish, grey mullet or mackerel, cleaned,
scaled and cut into 2.5cm/1in slices
1 hot seasoning pepper, seeded and finely chopped
2 garlic cloves, crushed
2 tablespoons finely chopped fresh chives
4 tablespoons fresh lime juice
1 teaspoon salt
2 tablespoons finely chopped fresh chives, to garnish

For the sauce
2 tablespoons butter
2 tablespoons olive oil
6 spring onions, trimmed and finely chopped
6 tomatoes, skinned and chopped
2 tablespoons finely chopped fresh parsley
2 tablespoons finely chopped fresh chives
salt and freshly ground black pepper
4 tablespoons fresh lime juice
175ml/6fl oz dry white wine
4 garlic cloves, crushed

Serves 4-6

1 Put the fish in a large glass or china dish; pour in enough cold water to cover. Add the seasoning pepper, garlic cloves, chives, lime juice and salt and set aside to marinate for 1 hour.

2 Make the sauce: heat the butter and oil together in a large heavy-based frying-pan. Add the spring onions and cook for 3 minutes. Add the tomatoes, parsley and chives. Season to taste with salt and black pepper and cook for 5 minutes, stirring frequently.

3 Pour over 300ml/½ pint cold water and bring to the boil. Lower the heat, cover the pan and simmer the sauce for 10 minutes.

4 Drain the fish and discard the marinade. Add the fish to the sauce, and cook for 10 minutes, turning the fish from time to time.

5 Pour over the lime juice and wine. Stir in the garlic and bring to the boil. Lower the heat slightly and simmer, uncovered, for 5 minutes. Taste and adjust the seasoning.

6 Remove from the heat and transfer to a warmed serving dish. Sprinkle over the chives and serve the fish immediately.

Fish Fillets in a Lime Sauce

Perfect for those who are watching their weight, this dish is both healthy and slimming.

900g/2lb fish fillets, plaice or sole, skinned
juice of 1 lime
salt and white pepper
2 tablespoons butter

For the sauce
300ml/½ pint chicken stock
grated rind of ½ lime
1 tablespoon cornflour
juice of 2 limes
2 egg yolks, lightly beaten
1 teaspoon sugar
1 tablespoon finely chopped fresh chives
pinch of ground ginger

To garnish
1 bunch fresh chives
1 lime, halved

Serves 4

1 Wash the fish fillets under cold water. Pat dry with absorbent paper. Rub the lime juice over the fillets and season with salt and pepper. Roll up the fillets.

2 Grease a large plate with a little of the butter then place the rolled-up fillets on the plate. Dot with the remaining butter. Cover with foil. Place the plate over a saucepan half-filled with boiling water, and steam the fish for 10-15 minutes until cooked.

3 Meanwhile make the sauce: put the chicken stock and lime rind into a saucepan. Bring to the boil. Lower heat and simmer for 5 minutes. Mix the cornflour with the lime juice, and add to the stock. Cook over low heat, stirring for 5 minutes.

4 Put the egg yolks and the sugar in a heatproof bowl and gradually pour over the stock, beating with a wooden spoon as you pour.

5 Place the bowl over a saucepan half-filled with simmering water and cook, stirring, for 5-10 minutes, until sauce thickens. Add ginger and season to taste.

6 Transfer fish to a heated serving platter. Pour over the sauce and garnish with chives and lime halves.

Fish Pie

The sweet potato topping on this Fish Pie provides the perfect contrast to the savoury fish filling.

100g/4oz butter
2 tablespoons oil
1 large onion, finely chopped
450g/1lb white fish fillets, cod or haddock, skinned
225g/8oz salt cod, soaked, skinned and shredded
2 hard-boiled eggs, chopped
700g/1½lb sweet potatoes
salt and freshly ground black pepper
4 tablespoons milk

For the sauce
40g/1½ oz butter
2 tablespoons flour
300ml/½ pint milk
100g/4oz Cheddar or Swiss cheese, grated
1 teaspoon curry powder
2 tablespoons finely chopped fresh parsley

Serves 6

1 Melt 25g/1oz of the butter with the oil in a large frying-pan over moderate heat. Add the onion and fry for 5 minutes. Add the fish and cook for 8-10 minutes. Remove pan from heat and stir in the eggs. Transfer to an ovenproof dish and set aside.

2 Boil the sweet potatoes in salted water for 20 minutes or until soft. Drain, rinse under cold water and peel. Put in a bowl and mash until smooth with 50g/2oz of the butter and the milk. Season to taste.

3 Heat the oven to 180C/350F/Gas 4.

4 Make the sauce: melt the butter in a saucepan, sprinkle in the flour and stir over low heat for 2 minutes. Off the heat gradually stir in the milk. Return pan to heat and bring to the boil. Lower heat and simmer, stirring constantly for 2-3 minutes. Add cheese, curry powder and parsley. Season to taste. Cook for 3-4 minutes more until sauce is thick.

5 Pour the sauce over the fish and mix well. Spoon the sweet potato over. Dot with remaining butter and cook in oven for 30 minutes, until golden.

Fish Fillets in a Lime Sauce (front) and
Martinique Poached Fish

Fish Steaks with Orange and Anchovy Butter

The fish called dolphin in the Caribbean bears no resemblance to the friendly dolphin or porpoise!

4 fish steaks, each weighing 225g/8oz, tuna or dolphin

For the marinade
2 garlic cloves, crushed
1 fresh chilli, seeded and finely chopped
1 onion, grated
2 tablespoons fresh lime juice
2 tablespoons olive oil
2 teaspoons dried thyme
1 teaspoon salt
freshly ground black pepper

For the butters
75g/3oz butter, softened
1 teaspoon grated orange rind
1 teaspoon dried thyme
1 teaspoon finely chopped fresh chives
4 anchovy fillets, rinsed and mashed

To garnish
4 orange slices
4 anchovy fillets, rolled

Serves 4

1 Wash the fish steaks and pat dry on absorbent paper. Place in a shallow china or glass dish.

2 Make the marinade: mix the garlic, chilli, onion, lime juice, olive oil, thyme, salt and pepper together. Pour over the fish and set aside to marinate for at least 2 hours or overnight, turning from time to time.

3 Make the butters: blend 40g/1½oz of the butter with the orange rind, thyme and chives in a small bowl. Shape into a small roll about 2.5cm/1in in diameter. Blend the remaining butter with the mashed anchovy and make a roll in the same way. Cover with cling film and freeze for 30 minutes.

4 Remove the butters from the freezer and cut each one into 4 slices. Place on a plate, cover with cling film and chill in the refrigerator until required.

5 Heat the grill or barbecue to high.

6 Remove the fish steaks from marinade, put on grill pan or barbecue grid and cook for 8-10 minutes, or until cooked through and golden brown on each side, brushing with the marinade.

7 Put fish on a warmed serving dish, garnished with the orange butter on the orange slices and the rolled anchovies on the anchovy butter. Serve immediately.

Fried Flying Fish

450g/1lb flying fish fillets, skinned
1½ teaspoons salt
juice of 1 lime
1 garlic clove, crushed
1 teaspoon finely chopped fresh chives
1 small onion, grated
½ teaspoon dried marjoram
dash of Tabasco
6 tablespoons flour
⅛ teaspoon cayenne pepper
freshly ground black pepper
1 egg, lightly beaten
oil, for frying
2 limes, cut into quarters, to garnish

Serves 4

1 Put the fish fillets into a shallow glass or china dish, season with 1 teaspoon salt and the lime juice and set aside for 15 minutes.

2 Drain and pat dry on absorbent paper. In a small bowl, mix the garlic, chives, onion, marjoram and Tabasco together. Rub the mixture into the fillets.

3 Mix the flour, cayenne pepper, ½ teaspoon salt and black pepper together in a shallow bowl. Place the beaten egg in another bowl. Dip the fillets first into the egg then into the seasoned flour.

4 Heat the oil in a heavy-based frying-pan and fry the fillets, a few at a time, for 3 minutes on each side. Keep warm while frying the remaining fillets.

5 Serve at once, garnished with lime quarters.

Fish Loaf

An interesting and economical dish, Fish Loaf is ideal for picnics. Serve with crusty French bread, a crisp green salad and lashings of home-made mayonnaise.

1 tablespoon butter, plus 1 teaspoon, for greasing
450g/1lb white fish fillets, cod, haddock, snapper or
grouper, skinned
1 tablespoon fresh lime juice
2 onions
1 bay leaf
2 whole cloves
salt and freshly ground black pepper
1 teaspoon whole black peppercorns
1 tablespoon flour
300ml/½ pint milk
2 eggs, beaten
2 hard-boiled eggs, chopped
2 tablespoons capers
2 tablespoons finely chopped gherkins
2 tablespoons finely chopped fresh parsley
100g/4oz fresh breadcrumbs
parsley sprigs, to garnish

Serves 4-6

1 Lightly grease a 600ml/1 pint loaf tin with the 1 teaspoon of butter.

2 Put the fish in a saucepan, add the lime juice and pour over enough cold water to cover. Slice one of the onions and add with the bay leaf, cloves, 1 teaspoon salt and the black peppercorns. Bring to the boil over moderate heat. Lower the heat, cover the pan and simmer for 10 minutes or until the fish flakes easily when tested with a fork.

3 Drain the fish and discard the seasonings. Flake the flesh with a fork and set aside.

4 Heat the oven to 180C/350F/Gas 4.

5 Heat the 1 tablespoon butter in a saucepan, sprinkle in the flour and cook, stirring constantly, for 2 minutes. Remove from the heat and gradually stir in the milk. Season with salt and pepper to taste.

6 Return the pan to the heat and cook over low heat, stirring constantly for 3-5 minutes, until the sauce coats the back of the spoon. Remove pan from heat.

7 Finely chop the remaining onion and add to the sauce. Stir in the flaked fish, beaten eggs, hard-boiled eggs, capers, gherkins, parsley and breadcrumbs. Season to taste with salt and pepper.

8 Spoon the mixture into the prepared tin. Cover with foil and cook in the oven for 45 minutes.

9 Remove from the oven and allow to cool. Cover with cling film then refrigerate overnight.

10 To serve, unmould the fish loaf by running a knife around the inside of the tin, then invert it on to a serving platter. Garnish with sprigs of parsley.

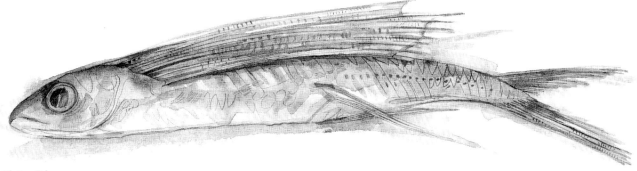

Flying fish

Stuffed and Baked Red Snapper

The red snapper in this recipe is wrapped in bacon before it is cooked to keep the fish succulent.

50g/2oz butter, melted
2 red snappers, each weighing 550g/1¼lb, cleaned
8 rashers streaky bacon
2 tablespoons olive oil
salt and freshly ground black pepper

For the stuffing
1 small onion, grated
75g/3oz mushrooms, wiped clean and finely chopped
75g/3oz ham, finely chopped
75g/3oz fresh breadcrumbs
1 teaspoon finely grated lemon rind
2 tablespoons finely chopped fresh parsley
1 teaspoon finely chopped fresh thyme
1 egg, lightly beaten

Serves 4

1 Heat the oven to 180C/350F/Gas 4.

2 Using 1 tablespoon of the melted butter, lightly grease a large, shallow ovenproof dish.

3 Make the stuffing: mix the onion, mushrooms, ham, breadcrumbs, lemon rind, parsley, thyme and egg together in a large bowl. Season to taste.

4 Enlarge the abdominal cavity of each fish to accommodate the stuffing. Stuff the fish with the mixture and secure the opening with cocktail sticks. Wrap 4 rashers of bacon around each fish.

5 Place the fish in the prepared ovenproof dish. Pour over the oil and remaining melted butter, and season.

6 Bake in the oven for 40-45 minutes, or until the fish flakes easily when tested with a fork, basting occasionally with the oil and butter.

7 Transfer to a warmed serving dish and serve the fish immediately.

Stewed Shark

Fish in the Caribbean is often rubbed with salt and lime before it is cooked, to 'cut the freshness' – a term used to describe the rather strong smell that fish tend to have in hot climates.

1kg/2lb 3oz shark, cut into 2.5cm/1in cubes
juice of 1 lime
1 teaspoon salt
1 tablespoon rum
3 tablespoons olive oil
100g/4oz salt pork, diced
2 large Spanish onions, finely sliced
3 garlic cloves, crushed
2 red peppers, seeded and finely sliced
350g/12oz can tomatoes, drained and chopped
225ml/8fl oz white wine
1 hot seasoning pepper
1 teaspoon dried oregano
1 tablespoon chopped fresh coriander
salt and freshly ground black pepper

Serves 6

1 Wash the fish cubes under cold water then rub them with the lime juice and salt to 'cut the freshness'. Rinse under cold water.

2 Place the fish in a bowl, pour over the rum and set aside for 10 minutes.

3 Heat the oil in a flameproof casserole. Add the diced salt pork and fry for 5 minutes until browned all over. Remove with a slotted spoon and drain on absorbent paper.

4 Add the onions to the pan and fry for 7 minutes until soft. Stir in the garlic and red peppers and fry for 5 minutes.

5 Drain the shark, reserving the liquid, and add the fish to the pan. Fry for 5 minutes, stirring frequently. Pour over the reserved liquid and add the tomatoes, white wine, seasoning pepper, oregano and coriander. Return the salt pork to the pan and season to taste with salt and pepper. Bring to the boil then simmer, covered, for 30 minutes, stirring frequently.

6 Serve straight from the casserole accompanied by Rice 'n' Peas (see page 80).

Stuffed and Baked Red Snapper

Crayfish and Rice Salad

A spectacular dish to serve at a dinner party or as part of a grand buffet, Crayfish and Rice Salad combines the delicate flavour of crayfish with the tropical tastes of pineapple, pawpaw and rice. Crayfish look very attractive with their bright orange colour and long claws but have very little flesh. If they are difficult to obtain or you wish for a more substantial shellfish, use either Dublin Bay prawns or small lobsters split in half.

1 onion, sliced
1 carrot, sliced
1 bay leaf
3 whole cloves
2.5cm/1in piece of fresh root ginger, peeled
1 teaspoon salt
freshly ground black pepper
1kg/2lb 3oz uncooked, unshelled crayfish (12 crayfish)
100g/4oz fresh young spinach, stems removed
¾ pineapple, peeled and sliced
1½ pawpaws, skinned, seeded and sliced

For the rice
450g/1lb long-grain rice, rinsed and drained
4 spring onions, trimmed and finely chopped
½ bunch watercress, trimmed and finely chopped
2 tablespoons finely chopped fresh parsley
2 tablespoons finely chopped fresh coriander
½ pawpaw, skinned, seeded and finely chopped
¼ pineapple, peeled and finely chopped
3 tablespoons oil
juice and grated rind of 1 orange
juice of 1 lime
10 whole young spinach leaves

For the mayonnaise
2 egg yolks
300ml/½ pint olive oil
1 tablespoon tomato ketchup
juice of ½ lime
1 garlic clove, crushed
salt

Serves 6

1 Put the onion, carrot, bay leaf, cloves and ginger into a large saucepan. Pour over 1.7l/3 pints of cold water. Add one 1 teaspoon salt and black pepper and bring to the boil over moderate heat. Lower the heat, cover the pan and simmer for 10 minutes. Carefully add the crayfish to the pan and bring back to the boil. Lower the heat and simmer for 5 minutes. Remove the pan from the heat, strain the liquid into a measuring jug and reserve. Refresh the crayfish under cold water. Discard the seasonings and set the crayfish aside to cool.

2 Put the rice in a pan, add 600ml/1 pint of the reserved liquid and bring to the boil over moderate heat. Lower the heat, cover the pan and simmer for 20 minutes until the rice is tender and the liquid has been absorbed. Remove from the heat, transfer to a mixing bowl and set aside to cool slightly.

3 Add the spring onions, watercress, parsley, coriander, pawpaw, pineapple, 2 tablespoons oil, orange juice and rind and the lime juice to the rice. Gently toss the ingredients together until they are thoroughly combined.

4 Grease a 1.7l/3 pint ring mould with the remaining oil. Line the mould with the spinach leaves, overlapping each one slightly. Spoon in the rice, smoothing the top with the back of a spoon. Cover with a plate and chill in the refrigerator for 1 hour.

5 Make the mayonnaise: whisk the egg yolks in a small bowl. Still whisking, add the oil, drop by drop, until it starts to thicken, then add the oil in a slow thin stream. When the mixture is thick, stir in the tomato ketchup, lime juice and garlic. Season to taste with salt and black pepper. Pour into a small bowl.

6 Line a large round serving platter with the spinach leaves. Remove the rice from the refrigerator and unmould on to the plate.

7 Put the bowl of mayonnaise in the centre of the rice (alternatively, spoon the mayonnaise into the centre). Arrange the sliced pineapple and pawpaws around the rice, then place the whole crayfish in a circle against the rice, with their tails just hanging over the plate. Serve immediately.

Stuffed Crabs
Crab Backs

Stuffed Crabs, or Crab Backs as they are called in Trinidad, make a most delicious supper party dish. Serve as a starter or as a main course accompanied by freshly baked rolls and a crisp green salad.

In the West Indies, Crab Backs are made with the small blue-backed land crabs that live in the mangrove swamps and coconut fields, however any other type of edible crab may be substituted, as available.

2 cooked crabs, each weighing approximately 700g/1½lb,
split open
2 tablespoons butter
1 onion, finely chopped
3 spring onions, trimmed and finely chopped
1 fresh chilli, seeded and finely chopped
2 tablespoons finely chopped fresh chives
2 teaspoons Worcestershire sauce
1 tablespoon fresh lime juice
2 tablespoons medium sherry or rum
pinch of grated nutmeg
1 teaspoon salt
freshly ground black pepper
100g/4oz fresh breadcrumbs

Serves 2-4

1 Clean the crabs: remove and discard the stomach, intestine, and the gills (dead man's fingers), and pick out all the crab meat from the shell, discarding any skin or cartilage. Reserve the shells. Crack open the claws and combine all the meat together in a large mixing bowl.

2 Heat the oven to 180C/350F/Gas 4.

3 Melt the butter in a frying-pan, add the onion and spring onions and fry, stirring constantly, over moderate heat, for 5 minutes, until soft and golden.

4 Remove from the heat and stir the onion and spring onions into the crab meat. Add the chilli, chives, Worcestershire sauce, lime juice, sherry or rum, nutmeg, salt, freshly ground pepper and 90g/3½oz breadcrumbs, then mix the ingredients thoroughly together.

5 Spoon the filling into the reserved shells and place on a baking sheet. Cook in the centre of the oven for 15 minutes.

6 Remove the crabs from the oven and sprinkle over the remaining breadcrumbs. Return to the oven and cook for a further 15-20 minutes, until golden brown. Serve hot.

Pepper Shrimp

A great dish to share with friends – all you need is a bowl for the shells and beer to put out the heat!

2 tablespoons olive oil
5 garlic cloves, crushed
2-3 fresh chillies, seeded and finely chopped
2 tablespoons fresh lemon juice
4 tomatoes, skinned and chopped
salt and freshly ground black pepper
1 tablespoon Pepper Wine (see page 95)
1kg/2lb 3oz unshelled giant prawns

Serves 6-8

1 Heat the oil in a wok or large heavy-based frying-pan. Add the garlic and chillies and stir-fry for 1 minute over moderate heat.

2 Stir in the lemon juice and tomatoes, and season to taste with salt and pepper. Cook for a further 5 minutes. Add the pepper wine and prawns and cook for 5 minutes, stirring constantly, to heat through.

3 Transfer contents of pan to a warmed serving dish and serve immediately.

Crab Gumbo

The word 'gumbo' is synonymous with okra. This thick soupy stew can be made with crab, meat, fish or poultry, but always has okra as a common ingredient. When buying okra choose the small firm pods and avoid the large dark green pods which tend to be rather stringy.

2 cooked crabs, each weighing 1kg/2lb 3oz, cleaned
2 tablespoons butter
1 tablespoon olive oil
1 Spanish onion, finely chopped
400g/14oz can tomatoes, drained and chopped
1 tablespoon finely chopped fresh thyme
2 tablespoons finely chopped fresh parsley
1 tablespoon finely chopped fresh chives
225g/8oz okra, trimmed and sliced
1 hot seasoning pepper
salt and freshly ground black pepper

Serves 4-6

1 Using a cleaver, cut off the legs and claws from the crab and crack with a nutcracker. Then cut the body into quarters.

2 Heat the butter and the oil together in a large saucepan over moderate heat. Add the onion and fry, stirring constantly for 5 minutes.

3 Add the crab and cook, turning frequently for 5 minutes. Stir in the tomatoes, thyme, parsley and chives and cook, stirring constantly for 5 minutes.

4 Add the okra and hot seasoning pepper and pour over 1.1l/2 pints boiling water. Season with salt and pepper to taste. Lower the heat, and simmer for 45 minutes, stirring occasionally.

5 Remove the hot seasoning pepper, transfer to a warmed soup tureen and serve immediately, ladling the gumbo into soup bowls.

Curried Prawns and Pineapple

Uncooked prawns or shrimps have much better flavour than the pink cooked ones. They are sold in specialist fishmongers and Chinese supermarkets. Monkfish makes an excellent substitute.

2 small pineapples
1 tablespoon butter
1 tablespoon oil
1 large onion, finely chopped
1½ tablespoons garam masala
¼ teaspoon ground saffron (or turmeric)
pinch of cayenne pepper
450g/1lb uncooked shelled giant prawns,
cut into 1.5cm/½in lengths
1 tablespoon fresh lemon juice
300ml/½ pint double cream
100g/4oz toasted almonds
salt and freshly ground black pepper

Serves 4

1 Cut the pineapples in half lengthways through the leaves. Using a small sharp knife, cut out the pineapple flesh, and chop into 1.5cm/½in cubes. Set aside. Place the hollowed-out pineapple halves on a large serving platter.

2 Melt the butter and oil together in a large frying-pan over moderate heat. Add the onion and fry for 5 minutes. Stir in the garam masala, saffron and cayenne pepper and cook for a further 2 minutes.

3 Add the prawns and lemon juice to the pan and stir-fry for 5 minutes. Pour over the cream, add the pineapple and half the almonds and season to taste with salt and black pepper. Cook for a further 5 minutes, stirring constantly.

4 Remove the pan from the heat and spoon the mixture into the reserved pineapple shells. Scatter over the remaining almonds and serve immediately.

Pepper Shrimp (front) and Crab Gumbo

Prawns and Rice
Arroz con Camarones

The combination of prawns with rice is another inter-island speciality, with each island in the Caribbean having its own version. This particular recipe reflects the Spanish influence in the cooking of the Caribbean.

3 tablespoons olive oil
1 large onion, finely chopped
2 spring onions, trimmed and finely chopped
3 garlic cloves, crushed
4 tomatoes, skinned and chopped
400g/14oz can pimentos, drained and sliced
2 tablespoons finely chopped fresh parsley
2 tablespoons finely chopped fresh coriander
350g/12oz medium-grain rice, rinsed and drained
salt and freshly ground black pepper
900ml/1½ pints chicken stock
1 hot seasoning pepper
400g/14oz can petits pois, drained
800g/1¾lb uncooked, unshelled prawns
2 tablespoons fresh lemon juice
1 avocado pear, to garnish

Serves 6

1 Heat the oil in a large heavy-based frying-pan. Add the onion and cook for 5 minutes over moderate heat. Stir in the spring onions, garlic and tomatoes and cook for 5 minutes, stirring constantly.

2 Add the pimentos, parsley, coriander and rice. Season to taste with salt and black pepper and cook for 2 minutes, stirring constantly. Pour over the chicken stock, add the seasoning pepper, and bring to the boil. Lower the heat, cover the pan and simmer for 15 minutes.

3 Carefully stir the peas and prawns into the rice, and cook for a further 10 minutes, turning the prawns frequently so that they cook evenly.

4 Pour over the lemon juice. Taste and adjust the seasoning. Transfer to a warmed serving dish. Peel and thinly slice the avocado. Garnish with the avocado slices and serve immediately.

Shrimp-filled Edam Cheese
Keshy Yena

One of the most interesting dishes of the Caribbean, Shrimp-filled Edam Cheese or Keshy Yena is a speciality from the Dutch island of Curaçao.

1.8kg/4lb whole Edam cheese, wax skin removed
1 tablespoon butter, for greasing

For the filling
1 tablespoon butter
6 spring onions, trimmed and finely chopped
1 fresh chilli, seeded and finely chopped
1 green pepper, seeded and finely chopped
350g/12oz shelled prawns
50g/2oz gherkins, chopped
50g/2oz sultanas
2 tomatoes, skinned and chopped
50g/2oz fresh breadcrumbs
1 teaspoon Worcestershire sauce
1 tablespoon sherry
1 egg, beaten
salt and freshly ground black pepper

Serves 6

1 Slice 2.5cm/1in off the top of the cheese to use for a lid. Carefully scoop out most of the cheese inside the lid and hollow out the whole cheese, leaving a 2cm/¾in thick shell. Grate the cheese and reserve.

2 Heat the oven to 180C/350F/Gas 4. Grease a shallow ovenproof dish with the butter.

3 Make the filling: melt the butter in a frying-pan, add the spring onions, chilli and green pepper and cook for 5 minutes over moderate heat, stirring constantly. Remove from the heat and stir in the prawns, gherkins, sultanas, tomatoes, breadcrumbs, Worcestershire sauce, sherry and egg. Add 175g/6oz of the reserved grated cheese, mix well together and season to taste with salt and black pepper.

4 Fill the cheese with the stuffing. Cover with the lid, then put in the ovenproof dish and cook in the centre of the oven for 30 minutes. (Do not over-cook or the cheese will become hard.)

5 Serve immediately from the dish, cutting the cheese into slices.

Seafood Pancakes

A rich and impressive dish for seafood lovers, these delicious pancakes can be made the day before and heated through and filled just before serving.

4 tablespoons oil, for frying

For the batter
225g/8oz plain flour
½ teaspoon salt
¼ teaspoon grated nutmeg
2 eggs, beaten
1 tablespoon oil
600ml/1 pint milk

For the filling
2 tablespoons oil
50g/2oz butter
1 onion, finely chopped
2 garlic cloves, crushed
225g/8oz crab meat
175g/6oz white fish fillets, cod, haddock or snapper,
skinned and cut into 2.5cm/1in cubes
225g/8oz shelled prawns
150ml/¼ pint white wine
2 tablespoons flour
300ml/½ pint milk
1 ripe avocado pear
175g/6oz Gruyère cheese, grated
⅛ teaspoon grated nutmeg
salt and freshly ground black pepper

To garnish
1 firm ripe avocado pear
1 lime, thinly sliced

Serves 6 (Makes 12 pancakes)

1 First make the batter: sift the flour, salt and nutmeg into a large mixing bowl. Make a well in the centre and add the beaten eggs, oil and 2 tablespoons of the milk. Beat together with a whisk, gradually drawing in the flour. Slowly pour in the remaining milk and 125ml/4fl oz water, and beat the mixture into a smooth batter. Leave to stand for 30 minutes.

2 Meanwhile make the filling: heat the oil with 25g/1oz butter in a large frying-pan over moderate heat. Add the onion and fry, stirring constantly for 5 minutes. Stir in the garlic and cook for 3 minutes.

3 Add the crab meat to the pan and stir-fry for 6 minutes. Add the fish, prawns and the white wine and cook for 10 minutes, stirring constantly, until the fish is cooked and most of the liquid has been absorbed. Remove from the heat and set aside.

4 Melt the remaining butter in a saucepan over moderate heat. Sprinkle over the flour and cook, stirring constantly, for 2 minutes.

5 Remove the pan from the heat and gradually add the milk, stirring constantly. Peel the avocado and mash to a purée, then stir into the sauce with the cheese and nutmeg. Season to taste.

6 Return to low heat and cook for 5 minutes, stirring constantly, until the mixture is thick enough to coat the back of the spoon. Stir in the seafood mixture and keep warm while you make the pancakes.

7 Heat a 20cm/8in frying-pan over moderately high heat. Pour in 1 teaspoon of the oil and wipe over the pan with absorbent paper. Pour in three-quarters of a ladle of the batter, tipping the pan as you pour, so the batter evenly coats the bottom.

8 Cook for approximately 30 seconds, until the surface sets and the bottom of the pancake is golden brown. Using a spatula, turn the pancake over and cook for 30 seconds. Keep warm in a low oven while you cook the remaining batter. Adjust the heat under the pan for each pancake.

9 Divide the mixture equally between each pancake and roll them up. Arrange on a warmed serving dish. Peel and thinly slice the avocado, then garnish with avocado and lime slices and serve immediately.

MEAT DISHES

Since chicken, pigs and goats are easy to rear in the Caribbean climate, they provide the most popular form of meat on most of the islands. However, some islands do breed beef cattle and lamb is imported. For those with a taste for wild game, there is plenty of local game still hunted; agouti, armadillo and even parrot are said to be eaten on some islands. All meat is either marinated and seasoned before it is cooked or highly seasoned during cooking, making it very tasty.

Chicken in Coconuts

A novel way to serve Chicken in Coconuts is to place the coconut halves on a bed of rice to prevent them from toppling over. The rice can be decorated with mango and sprigs of coriander.

3 coconuts, drained and liquid reserved
1 tablespoon butter
1 tablespoon olive oil
2 garlic cloves, crushed
1kg/2lb 3oz boned, skinned chicken,
cut into 2.5cm/1in cubes
1 onion, finely chopped
1 teaspoon finely chopped fresh ginger
1 tablespoon finely chopped fresh coriander
1 teaspoon salt
pinch of white pepper
1 tablespoon cornflour
150ml/¼ pint single cream
1 large firm ripe mango, peeled and diced
finely chopped fresh coriander, to garnish

Serves 6

1 Split the coconuts in half, scoop out the flesh and cut away the brown skin from half a coconut. Cut into thin slivers with a potato peeler and reserve. Make coconut milk using all the remaining coconut flesh (see page 16). Reserve 600ml/1 pint for this recipe (freeze the rest). Put the 6 coconut halves into a serving dish.

2 Heat the grill to moderate and sprinkle the slivered coconut into the grill pan. Toast under the grill for 5-10 minutes, shaking the pan frequently, until the coconut is golden brown. Transfer to a bowl and set aside.

3 Heat the butter and oil together in a saucepan. Add the garlic and cook for 1 minute. Stir in the chicken cubes and cook for 5 minutes, stirring frequently. Using a slotted spoon, transfer the chicken to a plate.

4 Add the onion and ginger to the pan and cook for 5 minutes. Pour in the coconut milk and coriander. Return the chicken to the pan, season with the salt and white pepper and bring to the boil. Lower the heat, cover the pan and simmer for 15 minutes.

5 Mix the cornflour with 3 tablespoons of the cream. Add the cornflour mixture, remaining cream and mango to the pan and cook for 2 minutes, or until the sauce is smooth and fairly thick. Stir in the toasted coconut and spoon the chicken mixture into the 6 coconut shells. Garnish with a sprinkling of finely chopped coriander.

Chicken in Coconuts

Chicken and Palm Heart Pie

This recipe came originally from South America, and through the years has been changed and adapted to the Caribbean islands. The pastry is very crumbly and has to be pieced together like a patchwork. It is a good dish to eat cold at picnics.

550g/1¼lb plain flour
pinch of salt
¼ teaspoon grated nutmeg
3 eggs, beaten
1 tablespoon melted butter
225-300ml/8-10fl oz oil, plus 1 teaspoon, for greasing
1 egg yolk, lightly beaten, for glazing

For the filling
2 tablespoons butter
2 tablespoons flour
300ml/½ pint milk
salt and freshly ground black pepper
1 bay leaf
1 tablespoon oil
1 large onion, finely chopped
2 garlic cloves, crushed
2 tomatoes, skinned and chopped
425g/15oz can palm hearts, drained and cut into
1.5cm/½in lengths
400g/14oz can petits pois, drained
350g/12oz boneless cooked chicken, skin removed and
flesh chopped into 1.5cm/½in cubes
2 tablespoons finely chopped fresh parsley

Serves 6

1 First make the filling: melt the butter in a saucepan over moderate heat. Sprinkle over the flour and cook, stirring constantly for 2 minutes.

2 Remove the pan from the heat and gradually add the milk, stirring constantly. Season to taste with the salt and pepper and add the bay leaf. Return to low heat and cook for 5 minutes, stirring constantly, until the sauce is thick enough to coat the back of the spoon. Remove the bay leaf and set aside.

3 Heat the oil in another saucepan, add the onion and fry over moderate heat for 5 minutes, until soft and golden. Stir in the garlic and tomatoes and cook for 3 minutes. Add the palm hearts, petits pois, chicken and parsley. Season to taste with salt and black pepper.

4 Stir the mixture into the sauce and set aside to cool completely.

5 Meanwhile make the pastry: put the flour, salt and nutmeg into a large mixing bowl. Make a well in the centre and add the eggs, butter and 225ml/8fl oz oil. Form the mixture into a dough with your hands, adding more oil if the mixture seems dry.

6 Heat the oven to 180C/350F/Gas 4. Lightly grease a 20 × 25cm/8 × 10in rectangular pie dish with the teaspoon of oil.

7 Roll out half the pastry on a floured surface until it is 5mm/¼in thick. Lift pieces of the crumbly pastry with a palette knife and piece them together in the pie dish, pressing the edges together. Completely line the pie dish then spoon in the chicken filling.

8 Roll out the remaining pastry in the same way and cover the filling, sealing the edges with your fingers. Roll out the pastry trimmings and decorate the top of the pie. Brush the top with the beaten egg yolk and place the pie in the centre of the oven for 45-60 minutes, until the pastry is golden brown.

9 Remove from the oven and serve immediately.

Chicken Fricassée

This French Creole chicken stew is one of the characteristic dishes of the Caribbean.

1.6kg/3½lb chicken, cut into 12 pieces
1 tablespoon oil
1 tablespoon brown sugar
2 onions, finely chopped
4 spring onions, trimmed and finely chopped
3 tomatoes, skinned and chopped
450ml/¾ pint chicken stock
1 hot seasoning pepper
1 bay leaf
2 tablespoons finely chopped fresh parsley, to garnish

For the marinade
juice of 1 lime
2 garlic cloves
1 teaspoon dried thyme
1 fresh chilli, seeded and finely chopped
1 tablespoon Worcestershire sauce
salt and freshly ground black pepper

Serves 6

1 Make the marinade: mix all the marinade ingredients together in a small bowl.

2 Put the chicken pieces in a large mixing bowl and pour over the marinade. Marinate for 2 hours, turning occasionally. Drain, reserving marinade.

3 In a large saucepan or flameproof casserole carefully heat the oil and sugar over moderate heat until the sugar begins to caramelize. Add half the chicken at a time and brown for 15 minutes, turning frequently. Remove with a slotted spoon.

4 Fry the onions and spring onions for 5 minutes in the oil remaining in the pan, stirring frequently.

5 Stir in the tomatoes and cook for 5 minutes. Pour over the stock and the reserved marinade, then add the seasoning pepper and bay leaf and bring to the boil. Return chicken to pan and lower heat. Simmer for 20-30 minutes, or until the chicken is tender. Taste and adjust seasoning.

6 To serve, transfer the chicken and sauce to a warmed serving dish, remove the seasoning pepper and bay leaf and garnish with parsley.

Banana and Rice Stuffed Chicken

The sweet stuffing of bananas and rice goes perfectly with the succulent flesh of the roast chicken. This recipe is an adaptation of a famous Haitian recipe where the chicken is flambéed in rum as it is served.

1.8kg/4lb chicken
1 teaspoon salt
¼ teaspoon white pepper
1 tablespoon clear honey
4 tablespoons fresh orange juice
watercress sprigs, to garnish

For the stuffing
175g/6oz cooked rice
3 ripe bananas, mashed
juice and grated rind of 1 large orange
1 tablespoon rum
2 tablespoons sultanas
pinch of ground ginger
pinch of grated nutmeg
salt and freshly ground black pepper

Serves 6

1 Heat the oven to 180C/350F/Gas 4.

2 Make the stuffing: mix the rice, bananas, orange juice and rind, rum, sultanas, ginger and nutmeg together. Season to taste with salt and black pepper.

3 Wash the chicken and dry with absorbent paper. Stuff the cavity of the chicken with the stuffing. Season the outside with the salt and white pepper and place in a roasting tin.

4 Mix the honey with the orange juice and pour over the chicken.

5 Roast in the oven for 1½ hours, basting occasionally, until the chicken is tender and cooked through when tested with a skewer.

6 Transfer to a warmed serving dish, garnish with watercress sprigs and serve immediately.

Chicken with Rice and Pigeon Peas
Chicken Pelau

Each island in the Caribbean has its own way of seasoning, depending upon which herbs grow locally. The seasoning herbs are generally combined with onion, garlic, sive or chives and sometimes a little hot pepper, then blended to a purée with a little water. The mixture is then kept in a screw-top jar in the refrigerator and used each day.

Chicken Pelau is a national favourite in Trinidad and Tobago. Most people will eat a pelau on a Sunday after coming back from the beach.

A good pelau must be brown – the secret lies in 'browning down' or caramelizing the chicken in a little oil and sugar to give it that rich brown colour.

½ coconut, chopped
liquid from the coconut
450g/16oz can pigeon peas, drained
1 hot seasoning pepper
1 teaspoon salt
freshly ground black pepper
2 tablespoons oil
2 tablespoons sugar
1.6kg/3½lb chicken, cut into 5cm/2in pieces
225g/8oz rice, rinsed and drained

For the seasoning
1 onion, chopped
2 garlic cloves
1 tablespoon chopped fresh chives
1 tablespoon chopped fresh thyme
2 celery stalks with leaves, chopped

Serves 6

1 Make the seasoning: put the onion, garlic, chives, thyme and celery into a food processor or blender with 4 tablespoons of water and process for 30 seconds until the mixture is puréed. Pour the seasoning into a pan and set aside while you make the coconut milk.

2 Rinse out the food processor or blender then add the chopped coconut with the coconut liquid and process to form a thick milk, adding more water if necessary. Pour into the saucepan, adding the pigeon peas and the seasoning pepper, and place over low heat for 15 minutes. Season with salt and black pepper.

3 In a heavy-based saucepan or flameproof casserole heat the oil and sugar together over moderate heat until the sugar begins to caramelize, taking care not to burn it. Add the chicken pieces and cook for 15-20 minutes, turning frequently, until they are browned all over.

4 Stir in the pigeon pea mixture and the rice, adding 300ml/½ pint of water. Bring to the boil, then reduce the heat to low, cover the pan and simmer for 20 minutes, until the chicken and rice are cooked.

5 Taste and adjust the seasoning. Discard the hot seasoning pepper before serving.

*Chicken with Rice and Pigeon Peas (front) and
Banana and Rice Stuffed Chicken*

Four-Stuffing Christmas Turkey

In the Caribbean the stuffing is as important as the turkey itself. Impress your family and friends at Christmas time with this Four-Stuffing Christmas Turkey. Two of the stuffings are hot and two are served together cold like a layered pâté.

6.8kg/15lb turkey, cleaned, washed and dried
1 teaspoon salt
freshly ground black pepper
225g/8oz butter, melted
reserved pineapple juice (see below)

For the Prune and Sausagemeat Stuffing
2 tablespoons grated onion
2 tablespoons finely chopped fresh chives
2 tablespoons finely chopped fresh parsley
350g/12oz pre-soaked pitted prunes, chopped
700g/1½lb sausagemeat
grated rind of 1 orange
1 tablespoon brandy
¼ teaspoon ground cloves
1 teaspoon salt

For the Pineapple and Herb Stuffing
1 large Spanish onion, finely chopped
6 spring onions, finely chopped
3 garlic cloves, crushed
350g/12oz fresh breadcrumbs
2 tablespoons chopped fresh thyme
2 tablespoons finely chopped celery
grated rind and juice of 1 lime
400g/14oz can pineapple cubes, drained and chopped,
juice reserved (see above)
1 egg, lightly beaten
1 teaspoon salt

For the Chicken Liver Stuffing
1 tablespoon butter
1 tablespoon olive oil
1 onion, finely chopped
3 garlic cloves, crushed
450g/1lb chicken livers, trimmed
100g/4oz cream cheese
½ teaspoon finely chopped fresh basil
1 tablespoon sherry
1 teaspoon salt
100g/4oz fresh breadcrumbs

For the Olive Stuffing
450g/1lb black olives, pitted and finely chopped
3 garlic cloves, crushed
50g/2oz butter
100g/4oz ground almonds

To garnish
225g/8oz pre-soaked pitted prunes
400g/14oz can pineapple rings, drained
watercress sprigs

Serves 12-14

1 Make the Prune and Sausagemeat Stuffing: mix the grated onion, chives, parsley, prunes, sausagemeat, orange rind, brandy, cloves, salt and some black pepper together in a large mixing bowl, until thoroughly combined. Set aside.

2 Make the Pineapple and Herb Stuffing: mix the onion, spring onions, garlic, breadcrumbs, thyme, celery, grated lime rind and juice, chopped pineapple, egg, salt and some black pepper together in a mixing bowl until they are thoroughly combined. Set aside.

3 Make the Chicken Liver Stuffing: heat the butter and the oil together in a small frying-pan. Add the onion and cook over moderate heat for 5 minutes, stirring frequently. Stir in the garlic and livers and cook for 8 minutes until the livers are browned on the outside and pink on the inside.

4 Remove from the heat and transfer to a food processor or blender. Add the cream cheese, basil, sherry, salt, some black pepper and breadcrumbs and process until the mixture forms a smooth purée. Set aside.

5 Make the Olive Stuffing: put the olives, garlic and butter into a food processor or blender and process to form a smooth purée. Stir in the ground almonds and spoon the mixture into the bottom of a terrine, smoothing down with the back of the spoon.

6 Spoon the chicken liver stuffing on top of the olive stuffing levelling surface with the back of the spoon. Cover the terrine and place in the refrigerator.

7 Heat the oven to 240C/475F/Gas 9.

8 Stuff the turkey with the Prune and Sausagemeat and the Pineapple and Herb Stuffings. Sew up the neck opening with a needle and thread.

9 Line a large roasting tin with two large sheets of foil, with enough overlapping to completely cover the turkey. Place the turkey in the tin and season with salt and pepper. Pour over half of the melted butter, pull up the foil to cover the turkey and fold over the edges to make a parcel.

10 Place in the oven and cook for 30 minutes.

11 Soak a thin piece of muslin in the remaining butter. Open the foil and cover the breast, legs and wings of the turkey with the muslin. Reseal the foil, lower the heat to 180C/350F/Gas 4 and cook for a further 3½ hours, basting frequently.

12 Fold back the foil, remove the muslin and pour over the reserved pineapple juice and cook for 30-45 minutes, basting frequently, or until the bird is golden brown and the juices run clear when a thigh is pierced with the point of a knife.

13 Remove the bird from the oven and transfer to a warmed platter. Garnish with the prunes and pineapple rings and allow to stand for 15 minutes before carving.

14 Meanwhile, remove the terrine from the refrigerator. Unmould the stuffings on to a large plate. Cut into 12-14 slices, garnish with the watercress and serve with the hot turkey.

Barbecued Chicken Wings

I first ate this dish at a midnight barbecue on a beach in Barbados. It tastes just as good at midday on a hibachi at home and is a favourite with children.

12 chicken wings

For the marinade
125ml/4fl oz soy sauce
50ml/2fl oz tomato ketchup
50ml/2fl oz vinegar
50ml/2fl oz honey
1 teaspoon ground ginger
freshly ground black pepper

Serves 4-6

1 Make the marinade: put the soy sauce, tomato ketchup, vinegar, honey, ginger and black pepper into a bowl and mix well.

2 Wash the chicken wings and remove any feathers. Place in a glass or china dish. Pour over the marinade, ensuring that all the wings are coated with the mixture. Cover with cling film and refrigerate for at least 2 hours or overnight.

3 Heat the oven to 180C/350F/Gas 4. Transfer the wings to an ovenproof dish, pour over the marinade and cook in the oven for 30 minutes, turning the wings after 15 minutes.

4 Heat the grill or barbecue to moderate.

5 Remove the wings from the oven, drain the marinade and reserve. Place the wings on the grill pan or barbecue grid and cook for 5-10 minutes, brushing with the reserved marinade, until brown and crispy.

6 Transfer to a warmed serving platter and serve the chicken immediately.

Caribbean Kebabs

A delicious combination of sweet and savoury, these kebabs should be served with Rice 'n' Peas (see page 80) and Okra in Spicy Tomato and Garlic Sauce (see page 82). Mangoes and pawpaws can be used instead of the bananas.

450g/1lb pork chops, trimmed of fat and cut into
4cm/1½in cubes
3 large bananas
12 rashers streaky bacon
425g/15oz can pineapple cubes, drained and
juice reserved (see below)
1 green pepper, seeded and cut into 4cm/1½in cubes
1 red pepper, seeded and cut into 4cm/1½in cubes

For the marinade
1 tablespoon honey
1 tablespoon soy sauce
2 garlic cloves, crushed
reserved pineapple juice (see above)
dash of Angostura bitters

Serves 6

1 First make the marinade: mix the honey, soy sauce, garlic, pineapple juice and Angostura bitters together.

2 Place the pork cubes in a glass or china dish and pour over the marinade. Set aside to marinate for at least 2 hours or overnight, turning occasionally.

3 Drain the pork cubes and reserve the marinade.

4 Cut the bananas into 4 equal lengths. Then roll each piece in a rasher of bacon.

5 Heat the grill to high.

6 Thread 6 long kebab skewers with alternate pieces of red pepper, pork, green pepper, pork, pineapple, banana and so on, putting 2 pieces of banana on each skewer.

7 Line a grill pan with foil and place the skewers in the pan. Brush the skewers with the reserved marinade and cook under the grill for 10 minutes, turning from time to time, and brushing frequently with the marinade, until the meat is cooked.

8 Transfer to a warmed serving platter and serve the kebabs immediately.

Pork with Aubergines

Pork with Aubergines is characteristic of the East Indian influence in West Indian cooking. Local names for aubergines may include melongene, garden egg or eggplant.

3 tablespoons oil
2 tablespoons sugar
450g/1lb stewing pork, cut into 2.5cm/1in cubes
1 onion, finely chopped
2 garlic cloves, crushed
2 teaspoons ground cumin
450g/1lb aubergines, cut into 2.5cm/1in cubes
450g/1lb potatoes, peeled and cut into 2.5cm/1in cubes
1 teaspoon salt
freshly ground black pepper
600ml/1 pint chicken stock

Serves 6

1 Heat 2 tablespoons of the oil with the sugar in a flameproof casserole over moderate heat until the sugar begins to caramelize. Be careful not to let the sugar burn.

2 Add the pork cubes and cook for 6-8 minutes, stirring constantly, until they are golden brown. Remove with a slotted spoon and set aside.

3 Pour the remaining oil into the pan, add the onion and fry, stirring constantly, over moderate heat for 3-5 minutes.

4 Add the garlic, cumin, aubergines and potatoes. Season with salt and pepper and cook for 5 minutes. Return the pork to the casserole, pour over the stock and bring to the boil. Lower the heat, cover the casserole and simmer, stirring occasionally, for 1 hour until tender.

5 Taste and adjust seasoning. Serve at once straight from the casserole.

Caribbean Kebabs (front) and Pineapple Spare Ribs

Guava Pork Chops

Guavas are one of the most common fruit of the West Indies. When ripe they have a distinctive smell and exotic flavour. They may be eaten raw but are best stewed or made into jelly or guava cheese (a compressed pulp).

4 large pork chops
1 teaspoon dried rosemary
2 garlic cloves
salt and freshly ground black pepper
juice of 1 lemon
2 tablespoons guava jelly
400g/14oz can guavas, drained and juice reserved
1 tablespoon cornflour
parsley sprigs, to garnish

For the stuffing
1 small onion, grated
50g/2oz fresh breadcrumbs
1 teaspoon dried rosemary
1 tablespoon finely chopped fresh parsley
1 tablespoon rum
1 tablespoon butter

Serves 4

1 Season the chops with the rosemary, garlic, salt and pepper and set aside.

2 Put the lemon juice, guava jelly and the reserved guava juice in a small saucepan. Place the pan over low heat and cook, stirring constantly for 2 minutes, until the jelly has melted. Set aside.

3 Heat the grill to moderate.

4 Make the stuffing: mix the onion, breadcrumbs, rosemary, parsley and rum together. Season to taste with salt and pepper.

5 Using a teaspoon, scoop out and discard the pips from the centre of 4 guava halves. Fill the cavities with the stuffing and dot each one with a little of the butter.

6 Line a grill pan with foil and place the chops and the guavas in the pan. Brush a little of the guava juice over the chops and cook for 10 minutes on each side, brushing frequently with the juice.

7 Remove the guavas after the first 10 minutes, transfer to a serving dish and keep warm in a very low oven.

8 Turn the grill to high and cook the chops for about 5 more minutes on each side, until they are golden brown.

9 Transfer the chops to the serving dish and keep warm in the oven while you make the sauce.

10 Pour the cooking juices from the grill pan into the melted jelly mixture. Blend the cornflour with 3 tablespoons of the mixture in a small bowl. Add to the pan and bring to the boil over moderate heat, stirring constantly. Lower the heat and cook for 1 minute, until the sauce has thickened. Remove from the heat and pour over the chops. Garnish with parsley and serve immediately.

Jerked Pork Chops

Jerked Pork is one of the most famous of the traditional Jamaican dishes. It is thought to have originated from the Caribs and Arawaks and the tradition was carried on by the Maroons (the runaway slaves) who would season and spice a whole pig then roast it over freshly cut twigs.

4 pork chops
parsley sprigs or fresh coriander, to garnish

For the paste
6 spring onions, trimmed and chopped
1 teaspoon finely chopped, seeded hot seasoning pepper
1 teaspoon ground cinnamon
½ teaspoon grated nutmeg
½ teaspoon ground allspice
½ teaspoon ground cloves
1 bay leaf, crumbled
1 tablespoon olive oil
1 teaspoon salt
freshly ground black pepper

Serves 4

1 Make the paste: put the spring onions, seasoning pepper, cinnamon, nutmeg, allspice, cloves, bay leaf, olive oil, salt and pepper into a food processor or blender and process for 30 seconds until they form a smooth purée. Alternatively, pound them together with a pestle and mortar.

2 Put the pork chops in a large shallow china or glass dish and rub them all over with the paste. Cover with cling film and refrigerate for at least 2 hours or overnight.

3 Heat the grill to high.

4 Place the chops on a grill pan and cook under the grill for 7-10 minutes on each side.

5 Transfer to a warmed serving platter, garnish with the parsley sprigs or coriander leaves and serve the chops immediately.

Pineapple Spare Ribs

Molasses is used a great deal in the Caribbean, being a by-product of sugar cane. The molasses in this recipe gives the ribs a distinctive flavour and rich brown colour.

1kg/2lb 3oz pork barbecue spare ribs, trimmed
125ml/4fl oz malt vinegar
4 tablespoons cornflour
2 tablespoons molasses
125ml/4fl oz oil

For the sauce
425g/15oz can pineapple cubes
2 tablespoons honey
2 tablespoons Demerara sugar
225ml/8fl oz malt vinegar
1 red pepper, seeded and cut into 2.5cm/1in diamonds

Serves 4-6

1 Cut the spare ribs into individual ribs, then using a cleaver cut each rib in half.

2 Put the ribs in a saucepan, pour over the vinegar and 1.1l/2 pints of water. Bring to the boil over moderate heat, then lower the heat and simmer for 15 minutes. Drain, and cool slightly.

3 Mix the cornflour and molasses together in a large mixing bowl, add the ribs and coat them with the mixture, using your fingers.

4 Heat the oil in a deep-sided frying-pan or wok. When the oil is hot, add the ribs a few at a time and fry for 5 minutes, until golden brown. Remove with a slotted spoon and transfer to a plate while frying the remaining ribs.

5 Make the sauce: drain the pineapple cubes and pour the juice into a large saucepan. Add the honey, sugar, vinegar and 225ml/8fl oz water and heat slowly until the honey and sugar have dissolved.

6 Add the spare ribs and bring to the boil. Lower the heat, cover the pan and simmer gently for 30 minutes, turning the ribs frequently. Add the pineapple cubes and red pepper and cook for 5 minutes to heat through.

7 Transfer the contents of the pan to a warmed serving dish and serve immediately.

Beef and Okra Stew
Beef Gumbo

Okra combined with coconut gives this stew a rich and tasty sauce. Serve Beef and Okra Stew with plain boiled rice and an orange and cucumber salad.

Okra is a popular vegetable in Caribbean cooking. When cooked, the pods become sticky and syrupy and are used to thicken soups and stews.

450g/1lb stewing beef, cut into 2.5cm/1in cubes
salt and freshly ground black pepper
½ teaspoon ground mace
5 tablespoons oil
225g/8oz okra, trimmed
1 onion, finely chopped
2 garlic cloves, crushed
4 tomatoes, skinned and chopped
225ml/8fl oz coconut milk (see page 16)

To garnish
cherry tomatoes (optional)
coriander sprigs

Serves 4

1 Wipe the meat, and dry on absorbent paper. Season with ½ teaspoon salt, pepper and the mace.

2 Heat 2 tablespoons oil in a flameproof casserole. Add meat and fry for 6 minutes, stirring frequently, until browned. Remove with a slotted spoon.

3 Wipe out the casserole and add 2 tablespoons oil. Add the okra and fry for 5 minutes until brown, stirring frequently. Remove with a slotted spoon.

4 Heat the remaining oil in the casserole and gently fry the onion and garlic over low heat for 5 minutes until soft and golden. Add the tomatoes and cook for 3 minutes, stirring constantly.

5 Return the meat and okra to the casserole, pour in the coconut milk and 225ml/8fl oz water. Season with salt and pepper to taste and bring to the boil. Lower the heat, cover the casserole and simmer for 2 hours or until the meat is tender.

6 Transfer to a warmed serving dish, garnish with cherry tomatoes, if wished, and coriander sprigs. Serve immediately.

Minced Beef Hash
Picadillo

Minced Beef Hash or Picadillo as it is known in Cuba is traditionally served with a fried egg on top. Serve with Black Beans and Rice (see page 78).

2 tablespoons oil
2 onions, finely chopped
700g/1½lb minced beef
1 fresh chilli, seeded and finely chopped
2 garlic cloves, crushed
1 green pepper, seeded and chopped
1 red pepper, seeded and chopped
4 tomatoes, skinned and chopped
2 tablespoons finely chopped fresh parsley
½ teaspoon cumin seeds
2 teaspoons dried oregano
¼ teaspoon ground cloves
2 tablespoons sultanas
1 teaspoon salt
freshly ground black pepper
3 tablespoons stuffed green olives, chopped
2 tablespoons capers

To garnish
12 stuffed green olives, halved
coriander sprigs

Serves 6

1 Heat the oil in a large heavy-based frying-pan. Add the onions and fry over moderate heat for 6 minutes until golden brown.

2 Add the meat and cook, stirring constantly, for 10 minutes until lightly coloured.

3 Add the chilli, garlic, green and red peppers, tomatoes, parsley, cumin, oregano, cloves, sultanas, salt and black pepper, and cook for 15 minutes, stirring frequently.

4 Stir in the chopped olives and capers and cook for a further 5 minutes. Taste and adjust the seasoning. Transfer to a warmed serving dish, garnish with the halved olives and coriander sprigs and serve immediately.

Minced Beef Hash (front) and Beef and Okra Stew

Stuffed Baked Pawpaw

This recipe would traditionally be made with green pawpaws which are used as a vegetable in the Caribbean. The pawpaws in this version are ripe, providing a sweet contrast to the savoury stuffing. Unripe pawpaws contain an enzyme in the skin which may cause allergic reaction, so it is advisable to wear rubber gloves when handling them.

2 small pawpaws, total weight about 700g/1½lb, cut in half lengthways and seeded
1 lime, quartered, to garnish

For the filling
2 tablespoons oil
6 spring onions, trimmed and finely chopped
1 garlic clove, crushed
275g/10oz minced beef
1 fresh chilli, seeded and finely chopped
2 tomatoes, skinned and chopped
2 tablespoons sultanas
50g/2oz cashew nuts, toasted and chopped
2 tablespoons grated Parmesan cheese
1 teaspoon salt
freshly ground black pepper

Serves 4

1 Heat the oven to 180C/350F/Gas 4.

2 Make the filling: heat the oil in a frying-pan, add the spring onions and fry over moderate heat for 5 minutes, until soft and golden.

3 Add the garlic and cook for 2 minutes. Stir in the beef and fry for 6-8 minutes until brown.

4 Add the chilli, tomatoes, sultanas and cashew nuts and stir-fry for 5 minutes, or until most of the liquid in the pan has evaporated.

5 Remove the pan from the heat and stir 1 tablespoon of the cheese into the mixture.

6 Spoon the mixture into the pawpaw shells and place in a shallow roasting tin. Pour enough boiling water into the tin to come a quarter way up the pawpaws. Sprinkle over the remaining cheese and bake in the oven for 30 minutes.

7 Transfer to individual plates, and serve garnished with lime quarters.

Sweet and Sour Meat Balls

Pounding the meat makes these Sweet and Sour Meat Balls exceptionally light and a great family favourite.

700g/1½lb minced beef
100g/4oz fresh breadcrumbs
2 eggs, lightly beaten
1 onion, grated
1 teaspoon salt
freshly ground black pepper
4 tablespoons oil

For the sauce
3 celery stalks, thinly sliced
1 green pepper, seeded and thinly sliced
1 red pepper, seeded and thinly sliced
400ml/14fl oz malt vinegar
75g/3oz brown sugar
1 tablespoon soy sauce
½ teaspoon salt
1½ tablespoons cornflour mixed with 2 tablespoons water
425g/15oz can pineapple cubes, drained

Serves 6

1 Mix the minced beef, breadcrumbs, eggs, onion, salt and black pepper together in a large mixing bowl. Pound the mixture with the palm of your hand for 5 minutes. Shape into golf-ball size meat balls and set aside on a large plate.

2 Heat the oil in a large frying-pan over moderate heat. Add the meat balls, a few at a time, and fry for 6-8 minutes until they are golden brown, turning them frequently. Remove with a slotted spoon and set aside while frying the remaining meat balls.

3 Make the sauce: add the celery and peppers to the juices in the pan and cook for 5 minutes.

4 Mix the vinegar, sugar, soy sauce, salt, cornflour and 350ml/12fl oz water together in a bowl. Pour the mixture into the pan and bring to the boil, stirring constantly. Lower the heat and simmer for 3 minutes.

5 Return the meat balls to the pan together with the pineapple and cook for a further 20 minutes.

6 Transfer meat balls and sauce to a warmed serving dish and serve immediately.

Gingered Barbecued Lamb

Outdoor eating is a way of life in the Caribbean, and barbecues are a popular way of entertaining. This dish can be cooked to perfection on a barbecue as well as in the oven.

If using an uncovered barbecue, precook the meat in the oven following steps 1-5 for just 45 minutes, then transfer to the barbecue for the remaining cooking time, brushing frequently with the marinade.

Leg of pork can also be cooked in this way.

1.6kg/3½lb leg of lamb
4 garlic cloves, thinly sliced
5cm/2in piece of fresh root ginger, peeled and thinly sliced
watercress sprigs, to garnish

For the marinade
300ml/½ pint tomato ketchup
2 tablespoons clear honey
3 tablespoons Worcestershire sauce
1 teaspoon hot mustard
juice of ½ lemon or lime
⅛ teaspoon cayenne pepper
1 teaspoon salt
freshly ground black pepper

Serves 6-8

1 Make the marinade: put the tomato ketchup, honey, Worcestershire sauce, mustard, lemon or lime juice, cayenne pepper, salt, freshly ground black pepper and 175ml/6fl oz water into a small saucepan and bring to the boil, stirring constantly. Remove from the heat and set aside to cool.

2 Using a small sharp knife make small incisions all over the leg of lamb and push slivers of the garlic and ginger into the incisions.

3 Place the lamb in a large glass or china ovenproof dish, pour over the marinade and place in the refrigerator for at least 2 hours, turning the lamb once during this time.

4 Heat the oven to 190C/375F/Gas 5.

5 Roast the lamb in the dish with the marinade in the centre of the oven for 1½ hours, basting from time to time. If the sauce looks too thick add a little more water half-way through the cooking time.

6 Remove the lamb from the oven and transfer to a warmed serving dish. Garnish with watercress. Pour any excess oil from the remaining sauce in the pan, then pour into a serving bowl and serve separately.

Plantation Stew

Sancoche

This dish, sometimes served as a soup, was most probably created by slaves who, with their meagre ration, used their imaginations to create a tasty meal.

225g/8oz salt beef, cut into 2.5cm/1in cubes
225g/8oz salt pork, cut into 2.5cm/1in cubes
1 salted pig's tail, cut into cubes or sliced
4-5 tablespoons oil
250g/9oz stewing beef, cut into 2.5cm/1in cubes
2 onions, chopped
225g/8oz lentils or split peas, rinsed and drained
225g/8oz green bananas, peeled and cut into 2.5cm/1in slices
225g/8oz yam, peeled and cut into 2.5cm/1in slices
225g/8oz sweet potatoes, peeled and cut into 2.5cm/1in slices
100g/4oz okra, trimmed
1 hot seasoning pepper
1 teaspoon salt
freshly ground black pepper

Serves 6

1 Put the salt beef, salt pork and salted pig's tail in a large bowl. Pour over enough cold water to cover and leave to soak for 1 hour. Drain and pat the meat dry with absorbent paper.

2 Heat 2 tablespoons of the oil in a large saucepan or casserole and fry the salt beef for 6-8 minutes, stirring frequently, until it is lightly coloured on all sides. Remove with a slotted spoon and transfer to a plate while browning the remaining meat, adding more oil if necessary. Set aside.

3 Add 2 tablespoons of oil to the fat in the pan and fry the onions over moderate heat for 5 minutes.

4 Return the meat to the pan, add the lentils or split peas and pour over 600ml/1 pint water. Bring to the boil over moderate heat, lower the heat, cover the pan and simmer for 1½ hours.

5 Add all the remaining ingredients and cook for a further 20-30 minutes until tender.

6 Remove the seasoning pepper and transfer to a warmed serving dish.

Curried Lamb with Lentils

This fairly dry lamb curry is often made with goat and is popular in Trinidad as a spicy filling for roti (Indian bread).

2 tablespoons oil
1½ tablespoons cumin seeds
1 teaspoon turmeric
1 large onion, finely chopped
2 garlic cloves, crushed
1 fresh chilli, seeded and chopped
5cm/2in piece of fresh root ginger, peeled and finely chopped
1kg/2lb 3oz neck fillets of lamb, cut into 2.5cm/1in cubes
225g/8oz lentils, rinsed and drained
400g/14oz can tomatoes, drained and chopped
1 teaspoon salt
freshly ground black pepper

Serves 4-6

1 Heat the oil in a flameproof casserole, add the cumin and turmeric and fry over moderate heat for 1 minute, stirring constantly.

2 Add the onion and cook for 5 minutes. Stir in the garlic, chilli and fresh ginger and cook for a further 2 minutes.

3 Add the lamb and cook for 6-8 minutes until coloured, stirring constantly. Stir in the lentils, tomatoes, salt and black pepper. Pour over 600ml/1 pint cold water and bring to the boil. Lower the heat, cover the casserole and simmer for 1 hour. Remove the lid from the casserole and continue to cook, uncovered, for a further 30 minutes, stirring occasionally, until the lamb is tender and the sauce is thick.

4 Taste and adjust the seasoning. Remove from the heat and serve immediately.

Plantation Stew

Stuffed Rolled Plantains
Piononos

This Puerto Rican dish is traditionally served with Rice 'n' Peas (see page 80).

25g/1oz butter
165ml/5½fl oz oil
3 ripe plantains, peeled and cut into 4 long strips
2 eggs, lightly beaten

For the filling
1 tablespoon olive oil
1 small onion, finely chopped
1 garlic clove, crushed
450g/1lb minced beef
50g/2oz ham, finely chopped
2 tomatoes, skinned and diced
½ green pepper, seeded and finely chopped
6 olives, stoned and finely chopped
1 tablespoon capers, finely chopped
1 tablespoon sultanas, finely chopped
salt and freshly ground black pepper

Serves 6

1 Heat the butter and 1 tablespoon of the oil together in a frying-pan over moderate heat. Add the sliced plantains and fry, a few at a time, for 3-5 minutes until golden brown, turning once. Using a slotted spoon, transfer on to absorbent paper. Curve into rings, securing with wooden cocktail sticks.

2 Make the filling: heat the oil in a frying-pan, add the onion and fry for 5 minutes over moderate heat. Add garlic and beef and cook for 5-10 minutes. Add remaining filling ingredients, and season. Cook for a further 10 minutes, stirring frequently.

3 Fill each plantain ring with equal amounts of the meat mixture, smoothing the top of each ring flat.

4 Put the beaten eggs into a shallow bowl and dip each ring into the egg, coating all sides.

5 Heat the remaining oil in a heavy-based frying-pan and fry the plantain rings, a few at a time, for 2-3 minutes until golden brown. Using a slotted spoon, transfer the rings to absorbent paper to drain.

6 Place on a warmed dish and serve at once.

Goat Water

A simple stew from Montserrat, Goat Water should be served with plain boiled rice and steamed dasheen or spinach leaves. Goat meat is similar to lamb, though it is much maligned being thought of as tough and inedible. The meat of young kid is wonderfully delicate and can be favourably compared to that of spring lamb.

2 tablespoons oil
2 Spanish onions, chopped
2 garlic cloves, crushed
1kg/2lb 3oz goat meat, cut into 2.5cm/1in cubes
2 tablespoons tomato purée
4 whole cloves
1 bay leaf
1 teaspoon salt
freshly ground black pepper
1 tablespoon softened butter
1 tablespoon flour

Serves 4-6

1 Heat the oil in a large flameproof casserole, add the onions and fry for 6-8 minutes over moderate heat until soft and golden, stirring frequently.

2 Add the garlic and goat meat and cook for 10 minutes until lightly browned.

3 Stir in the tomato purée and pour in 900ml/1½ pints water. Add the cloves, bay leaf, salt and black pepper and bring to the boil. Boil for 10 minutes, skimming the scum that rises to the surface. Lower the heat, cover the casserole and simmer for 2¼ hours, stirring occasionally.

4 Mix the butter and the flour together in a small bowl to form a smooth paste. Stir the paste into the stew and cook, stirring constantly, for 2 minutes, until the sauce has thickened. Taste and adjust the seasoning and serve immediately.

Kidney Stew
Cocido de Rinones

This rich and tasty dish reflects the Spanish influence in Caribbean cooking.

8 lamb kidneys, skinned and excess fat removed
1½ teaspoons salt
2 tablespoons flour
freshly ground black pepper
¼ teaspoon curry powder
2 tablespoons oil

For the sauce
2 tablespoons oil
1 large Spanish onion, finely chopped
3 garlic cloves, crushed
4 rashers streaky bacon, diced
100g/4oz button mushrooms, wiped clean and trimmed
2 tablespoons finely chopped fresh coriander
300ml/½ pint chicken stock
4 tablespoons rum
4 tablespoons fresh orange juice
salt

Serves 4

1 Slice the kidneys in half lengthways and place in a bowl. Pour over enough cold water to cover and add 1 teaspoon of salt. Leave to soak for 10 minutes. Drain, then pat dry with absorbent paper.

2 Make the sauce: heat the oil in a medium saucepan. Add the onion and fry over moderate heat for 6 minutes, or until soft and golden.

3 Stir in the garlic and bacon and cook for 5 minutes. Then add the mushrooms and coriander and cook for 3 minutes. Pour over stock and bring to the boil. Lower heat and simmer for 15 minutes.

4 Meanwhile, mix the flour, ½ teaspoon salt, black pepper and curry powder together in a bowl. Toss the kidneys in the seasoned flour.

5 Heat the oil in a frying-pan and fry kidneys over moderate heat for 5 minutes, stirring constantly. Add the kidneys to the sauce, pour over the rum and orange juice, and cook for a further 5 minutes.

6 Transfer to a warmed serving dish and serve.

Mixed Meat Salad
Salpicon

Mixed Meat Salad or Salpicon is a well-known Cuban dish. This simple salad looks quite impressive when assembled, making a colourful dish for a cold buffet.

225g/8oz cold roast beef, diced
225g/8oz cold roast chicken, diced
225g/8oz cold honey roast ham, diced
450g/1lb new potatoes, scrubbed, boiled and sliced
175g/6oz can pineapple cubes, drained
1 red pepper, seeded and diced
3 large gherkins, diced
4 spring onions, trimmed and finely chopped
4 celery stalks, diced
2 tablespoons finely chopped fresh parsley
½ Iceberg lettuce, finely shredded
½ red pepper, seeded and thinly sliced, to garnish

For the dressing
1 teaspoon sugar
1 teaspoon prepared mustard
pinch of cayenne pepper
3 tablespoons white wine vinegar
8 tablespoons olive oil
salt and freshly ground black pepper

Serves 6

1 Make the dressing: mix the sugar, mustard and cayenne pepper together in a bowl. Add the vinegar then gradually whisk in the oil. Season to taste with salt and pepper.

2 In a large bowl, mix together the beef, chicken, ham, potatoes, pineapple, red pepper, gherkins, spring onions, celery and parsley. Pour over the dressing and toss the ingredients, ensuring they are completely coated.

3 Cover a large platter with the shredded lettuce.

4 Spoon the dressed salad on to the platter, building it into a mound. Garnish with the sliced red pepper and serve immediately.

VEGETABLE DISHES AND RELISHES

Vegetables play an important role in the planning of Caribbean meals. West Indians love their staple vegetables and there are usually at least two starchy vegetable accompaniments to each main dish. Through the imaginative use of herbs and seasoning many of the rather bland starchy vegetables are transformed into exciting and tasty dishes in their own right. Curried Green Bananas (see page 81) and Yam Salad (see page 89) are just two examples. Today many of these West Indian vegetables are available in our own local markets. Try substituting sweet potatoes for ordinary potatoes, or christophene for marrow or courgettes, or perhaps serve nutty-flavoured Tannia Fritters (see page 74) as an extra vegetable accompaniment to the Sunday roast.

Stuffed Pumpkin with Cashew Nuts

Stuffed Pumpkin with Cashew Nuts is an ideal dish to serve at a vegetarian dinner party. The pumpkin acts as an edible casserole and will keep the stuffing warm once it has been taken out of the oven for up to half an hour.

1.6kg/3½lb whole pumpkin

For the filling
50g/2oz butter
1 large Spanish onion, finely chopped
4 spring onions, trimmed and chopped
1 fresh chilli, seeded and chopped
350g/12oz cashew nuts, toasted
100g/4oz fresh breadcrumbs
1 egg, lightly beaten
1 teaspoon salt
freshly ground black pepper
100g/4oz Cheddar cheese, grated

Serves 6-8

1 Cut off 5cm/2in from the top of the pumpkin in a zig-zag line and reserve for the lid. Scoop out the seeds and membrane with a spoon and discard.

2 Heat the oven to 180C/350F/Gas 4.

3 Make the filling: heat 25g/1oz of the butter in a large saucepan, add the onion and cook for 5 minutes. Stir in the spring onions and chilli and cook for a further 2 minutes, stirring frequently.

4 Stir in the cashew nuts, breadcrumbs, egg, salt, black pepper and Cheddar cheese.

5 Remove the pan from the heat and spoon the mixture into the pumpkin shell. Dot with the remaining butter, cover with the top of the pumpkin, place on a baking sheet and bake in the centre of the oven for 1½ hours.

6 Remove from the oven and transfer to a serving dish. Serve cut into wedges.

Stuffed Pumpkin with Cashew Nuts

Spinach and Okra Purée
Vegetable Callaloo

In the Caribbean this is often called a Vegetable Callaloo – Spinach and Okra Purée is made in the same way as the soup Callaloo (see page 14), but without the crab and just a small amount of stock.

1 tablespoon olive oil
1 large onion, finely chopped
2 garlic cloves, crushed
225g/8oz okra, trimmed and chopped
550g/1¼lb frozen spinach, thawed
75ml/3fl oz chicken stock
200ml/7fl oz coconut milk (see page 16)
1 teaspoon salt
freshly ground black pepper
dash of Hot Pepper Sauce (see page 95)

Serves 6-8

1 Heat the oil in a saucepan, add the onion and cook over moderate heat for 5 minutes. Stir in the garlic and okra and cook, stirring frequently, for 3 minutes.

2 Add the spinach and pour in the stock, coconut milk, salt, pepper and a dash of pepper sauce.

3 Bring to the boil, lower the heat, cover the pan and simmer for 20 minutes.

4 Taste and adjust the seasoning. Transfer to a warmed serving dish and serve immediately.

Ackee and Cheese Soufflé

An unusual and elegant dish, Ackee and Cheese Soufflé can be served either as a starter or as part of a vegetarian meal.

40g/1½oz butter, plus ½ tablespoon, for greasing
25g/1oz flour
200ml/7fl oz milk
5 eggs, separated
75g/3oz Gruyère cheese, grated
1 teaspoon salt
freshly ground black pepper
1 teaspoon Worcestershire sauce
¼ teaspoon prepared mustard
350g/12oz can ackees, drained and mashed to a purée

Serves 4-6

1 Heat the oven to 180C/350F/Gas 4.

2 Using ½ tablespoon of butter, lightly grease a 1.4l/2½ pint soufflé dish.

3 Melt 40g/1½ oz butter in a saucepan, sprinkle in the flour and stir over low heat for 2 minutes. Remove the pan from the heat and gradually stir in the milk. Return the pan to the heat, bring to the boil, lower the heat and simmer, stirring constantly for 2-3 minutes. Remove from the heat and allow to cool slightly before adding the egg yolks, one at a time, beating the mixture well.

4 Add the cheese, salt and pepper, Worcestershire sauce and mustard, then add the ackee purée.

5 Using an electric beater, whisk the egg whites until stiff, then fold carefully into the ackee mixture with a metal spoon. Pour the mixture into the prepared soufflé dish and bake in the oven for 30-35 minutes, until risen and lightly browned.

6 Remove from the oven and serve immediately.

Baked Christophenes au Gratin

A delicate French Creole dish from Martinique, flavoured with a hint of nutmeg. Christophene, also known locally as cho-cho and chayote, is a tropical squash the size and shape of a pear.

4 christophenes
salt
5 tablespoons fresh breadcrumbs

For the sauce
25g/1oz butter
1 tablespoon flour
300ml/½ pint milk
⅛ teaspoon grated nutmeg
½ teaspoon salt
freshly ground black pepper

Serves 4

1 Put the unpeeled christophenes in a large saucepan. Cover with water, add salt and bring to the boil. Cook for 25-30 minutes, or until tender when pierced with a knife. Drain and refresh under cold water.

2 When cool enough to handle, peel, quarter and cut out the seeds. Chop the flesh roughly then put in a food processor and process for 30 seconds, to form a rough purée. Turn the purée into a clean muslin cloth and squeeze tightly, to drain off the excess liquid. Set aside.

3 Heat the oven to 200C/400F/Gas 6.

4 Make the sauce: melt the butter in a saucepan, sprinkle in the flour and cook over low heat, stirring constantly, for 2 minutes. Remove the pan from the heat and gradually stir in the milk. Season with the nutmeg, salt and pepper.

5 Return the pan to the heat and bring to the boil. Lower the heat and simmer, stirring constantly, for 3-5 minutes, until the sauce is thick enough to coat the back of the spoon.

6 Remove the pan from the heat and stir in the christophene purée.

7 Spoon the mixture into a shallow ovenproof dish, sprinkle over the breadcrumbs and bake in the oven for 30 minutes.

Christophenes

73

Plantains Baked in Cheese Sauce

The riper the plantains the sweeter the taste. Plantains Baked in Cheese Sauce is a good dish to serve as part of a vegetarian meal or as a substantial vegetable accompaniment to barbecued meat.

3 tablespoons oil
1.4kg/3lb ripe plantains, peeled and sliced lengthways

For the sauce
50g/2oz butter
2 tablespoons flour
600ml/1 pint milk
1 bay leaf
¼ teaspoon grated nutmeg
1 teaspoon salt
freshly ground black pepper
225g/8oz Cheddar cheese, grated

Serves 6-8

1 Heat the oil in a large frying-pan. When the oil is hot, add the plantains, a few at a time, and fry for 1 minute until golden brown. Remove with a slotted spoon and transfer to absorbent paper to drain while frying the remaining plantains.

2 Heat the oven to 170C/325F/Gas 3.

3 Make the sauce: melt the butter in a saucepan, sprinkle in the flour and cook, stirring constantly for 2 minutes. Remove the pan from the heat and gradually stir in the milk. Add the bay leaf and season with the nutmeg, salt and black pepper.

4 Return the pan to the heat, stir in half the cheese and bring to the boil. Lower the heat and simmer, stirring constantly, for 3-5 minutes or until the sauce is thick enough to coat the back of the spoon. Remove the pan from the heat and set aside.

5 Place a layer of plantain in the bottom of an ovenproof dish, pour over half the sauce and sprinkle over half the grated cheese. Repeat with the remaining plantain and sauce, ending with a layer of grated cheese.

6 Bake in the centre of the oven for 1 hour; a lot of the sauce will have been absorbed into the plantains by this time.

7 Remove and serve immediately, from the dish.

Tannia Fritters

Tannia Fritters have a very distinctive slightly nutty flavour. The tannias are simply grated, seasoned, then deep-fried. Serve while they are still hot with drinks or as a vegetable accompaniment to Chicken Fricassée (see page 53).

1kg/2lb 3oz tannias
1 teaspoon salt
⅛ teaspoon grated nutmeg
freshly ground black pepper
175ml/6fl oz oil

Makes 24

1 Immerse the tannias in a saucepan of boiling water. Add the salt and continue boiling for 15 minutes. Drain and when cool enough to handle, peel and grate into a mixing bowl.

2 Season the grated tannia with the nutmeg, salt and black pepper and mix well together.

3 Heat the oil in a heavy-based frying-pan. When the oil is hot, drop tablespoons of the tannia mixture into the pan, a few at a time, and fry for 2-3 minutes or until they are golden brown.

4 Remove with a slotted spoon and drain on absorbent paper. Keep warm while frying the remaining fritters.

5 Transfer to a warmed serving dish and serve the fritters immediately.

Plantains Baked in Cheese Sauce (left) and Tannia Fritters

Breadfruit Oiled-down

This dish is usually made with salt meat or salt fish, sometimes both. The term 'oiled-down' refers to a dish that has been cooked with coconut milk until all the liquid has been absorbed, leaving a small amount of coconut oil in the bottom of the pan.

225g/8oz smoked gammon, diced
1 tablespoon oil
1 large onion, finely chopped
6 spring onions, trimmed and finely chopped
1 teaspoon dried thyme
900ml/1½ pints coconut milk (see page 16)
1.6kg/3½lb whole breadfruit, quartered and peeled
1 teaspoon salt
1 hot seasoning pepper (optional)

Serves 6-8

1 Put the gammon into a saucepan, cover with cold water and bring to the boil over moderate heat. Skim the scum that rises to the surface. Lower the heat, cover the pan and simmer for 20-30 minutes until tender. Drain and set aside.

2 Heat the oil in a large saucepan, add the onion, spring onions and thyme and cook for 5 minutes over moderate heat, stirring frequently.

3 Pour over the coconut milk and bring to the boil. Lower the heat, add the gammon, breadfruit, salt, black pepper and seasoning pepper, if using. Cover the pan and simmer for 30 minutes, or until the breadfruit is tender and the coconut milk has been absorbed, leaving only a thin film of coconut oil in the bottom of the pan.

4 Remove the seasoning pepper, taste and adjust the seasoning. Transfer to a warmed serving dish and serve immediately.

Candied Sweet Potatoes

The combination of orange juice, rum and sugar makes this dish something really special. For an attractive variation try combining white and orange sweet potatoes.

1kg/2lb 3oz sweet potatoes
40g/1½oz butter, plus 1 tablespoon, for greasing
3 tablespoons brown sugar
175ml/6fl oz fresh orange juice
2 tablespoons rum
⅛ teaspoon grated nutmeg

Serves 4-6

1 Put the unpeeled sweet potatoes in a large saucepan. Cover with cold water and bring to the boil over moderate heat. Boil for 20 minutes or until just tender. Drain and when cool enough to handle, peel and cut the sweet potatoes into slices about 1.5cm/½in thick.

2 Heat the oven to 180C/350F/Gas 4.

3 Using the 1 tablespoon butter, grease a large shallow ovenproof serving dish. Arrange the sliced sweet potatoes in the dish. Dot with the remaining butter and sprinkle over the sugar.

4 Pour over the orange juice and rum. Sprinkle over the nutmeg and bake in the oven for 30 minutes.

5 Remove from the oven and serve immediately.

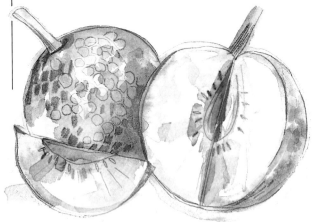

Breadfruit

Sautéed Topi Tambo

Topi tambo are root vegetables said to have been discovered in the Caribbean by the French colonists, who named them topin ambour. They are difficult to find outside the tropics but Jerusalem artichokes make a very good substitute.

450g/1lb even-sized topi tambo or Jerusalem artichokes,
washed and scrubbed
salt and freshly ground black pepper
2 tablespoons butter
1 tablespoon olive oil
2 garlic cloves, crushed
grated rind and juice of 2 lemons
2 tablespoons finely chopped fresh parsley
parsley sprigs, to garnish

Serves 4-6

1 Put the topi tambo or Jerusalem artichokes in a saucepan. Pour over enough cold water to cover. Add 1 teaspoon salt and bring to the boil over moderate heat. Boil for 8 minutes, remove from the heat and drain. Set aside.

2 Heat the butter and oil together in a large frying-pan over moderate heat. Add the garlic and fry for 1 minute.

3 Add the topi tambo or Jerusalem artichokes and fry, stirring constantly for 5 minutes. Stir in the lemon rind and juice and the parsley. Season to taste with salt and black pepper.

4 Transfer to a warmed serving dish, garnish with parsley sprigs and serve immediately.

Aubergines in Coconut Sauce

Canned coconut milk is particularly good for this dish, which is simple to make and a great favourite with anyone who likes aubergines.

700g/1½lb aubergines
1 tablespoon salt
6 tablespoons oil
2 tablespoons desiccated coconut

For the sauce
2 tablespoons oil
2 onions, sliced
2 garlic cloves, crushed
6 tomatoes, skinned and chopped
300ml/½ pint coconut milk (see page 16)
salt and freshly ground black pepper

Serves 6

1 Cut the aubergines into 1.5cm/½in slices and place in a colander. Sprinkle with 1 tablespoon salt and leave to degorge for 30 minutes. Rinse under cold water, then pat dry on absorbent paper.

2 Heat 2 tablespoons of the oil in a large frying-pan, add a third of the aubergines and fry for 10 minutes, turning once. Remove with a slotted spoon and drain on absorbent paper. Continue frying the remaining aubergines in two batches, using 2 tablespoons of oil for each batch.

3 Heat the oven to 180C/350F/Gas 4.

4 Make the sauce: heat the oil, add the onions and fry for 5 minutes over moderate heat, until soft and golden. Add the garlic and tomatoes and cook for 3 minutes, stirring constantly.

5 Pour in the coconut milk, season to taste with salt and black pepper and bring to the boil. Lower the heat and simmer the sauce for 5 minutes.

6 Layer the aubergines in an ovenproof dish and pour over the coconut sauce. Cover with foil and bake in the oven for 30 minutes.

7 Remove from the oven, sprinkle over the desiccated coconut then return to the oven and bake, uncovered, for a further 5-10 minutes, until the coconut is golden brown.

Black Beans and Rice
Moros y Cristianos

A Cuban speciality, this dish is called Moros Y Cristianos (Moors and Christians) in Spanish, referring to the black and white colour of the dish. Black beans have a strong almost meaty flavour and are used a great deal in Cuban cooking.

225g/8oz dried black beans
225g/8oz smoked gammon, trimmed of fat
and skin, then diced
2 tablespoons olive oil
1 onion, finely chopped
2 garlic cloves, crushed
2 tomatoes, skinned and chopped
1 green pepper, seeded and finely chopped
225g/8oz long-grain white rice, rinsed and drained
salt and freshly ground black pepper

Serves 6

1 Put the beans in a colander and pour over boiling water. Transfer to a large saucepan, add the diced gammon and cover with cold water. Bring to the boil over moderate heat and cook for 10 minutes, skimming off any scum. Lower heat, cover pan and simmer for 45-60 minutes, until beans are tender. Remove from heat and drain. Set meat to one side and refresh beans under cold water.

2 Heat the oil in a large saucepan, add the onion and fry for 5 minutes. Add garlic, tomatoes and green pepper and cook for 5 minutes, stirring constantly.

3 Add the rice, beans and gammon to the pan and season to taste. Pour in 600ml/1 pint of cold water and bring to the boil over moderate heat. Lower heat, cover pan and simmer for 20 minutes, until the rice is tender and the liquid has been absorbed.

4 Taste and adjust the seasoning. Transfer to a warmed serving dish and serve at once.

Creole Ratatouille

Serve as a perfect accompaniment to roast meat.

2 tablespoons olive oil
1 large onion, finely sliced
2 spring onions, trimmed and chopped
2 garlic cloves, crushed
1 fresh chilli, seeded and finely chopped
1 aubergine, peeled and cut into 2.5cm/1in cubes
1 red pepper, seeded and cut into 2.5cm/1in cubes
100g/4oz okra, trimmed and chopped
2 celery stalks, trimmed and chopped
1 christophene, peeled, seeded and chopped
400g/14oz can tomatoes, drained and chopped
1 teaspoon dried thyme
1 teaspoon finely chopped fresh basil
½ teaspoon brown sugar
salt and freshly ground black pepper
basil leaves, to garnish

Serves 4-6

1 Heat the oil in a flameproof casserole. Add the onion, spring onions and garlic and cook over low heat for 6 minutes, stirring constantly.

2 Stir in the chilli, aubergine, red pepper, okra, celery, christophene, tomatoes, thyme, basil and sugar. Season to taste with salt and black pepper. Pour in 450ml/¾ pint of cold water and bring to the boil over moderate heat. Lower the heat, cover the casserole and simmer for 45-60 minutes, stirring occasionally and adding more water if necessary.

3 Taste and adjust the seasoning, then garnish with basil. Serve hot or cold.

Creole Ratatouille (front) and Black Beans and Rice

Creamed Eddoes

Eddo, also known as taro, dasheen or 'old cocoyam', is a root vegetable belonging to the Arum family. The leaves are called dasheen or callaloo and are used to make the well-known soup of the same name.

450g/1lb eddoes
2 tablespoons butter
4 spring onions, trimmed and finely chopped
2 teaspoons fresh lime juice
225ml/8fl oz milk
¼ teaspoon Hot Pepper Sauce (see page 95)
salt and white pepper

Serves 4

1 Put the unpeeled eddoes in a saucepan. Cover with cold water and bring to the boil over moderate heat. Lower the heat, cover the pan and simmer for 20-30 minutes until tender. Drain and when cool enough to handle, peel off the skins.

2 Meanwhile, heat the butter in a saucepan, add the spring onions and cook for 3 minutes, stirring constantly over moderate heat until soft and golden.

3 Remove the pan from the heat and stir in the lime juice. Add the eddoes and the milk and mash to a purée with a potato masher.

4 Season the purée with the pepper sauce, salt and white pepper and spoon into a warmed serving dish. Serve immediately.

Rice 'n' Peas

Rice 'n' Peas is another inter-island speciality but it is generally associated with Jamaica, where it is traditionally served for Sunday lunch. The dish is in fact usually made with red kidney beans which are called 'peas' in Jamaica, but it can be made with fresh gungo (pigeon) peas.

175g/6oz dried red kidney beans, soaked in cold water
for 2 hours or overnight and drained
900ml/1½ pints coconut milk (see page 16)
1 sprig fresh thyme
1 hot seasoning pepper
4 spring onions, trimmed and finely chopped
2 garlic cloves, crushed
1 teaspoon salt
freshly ground black pepper
450g/1lb long-grain white rice

Serves 6-8

1 Put the beans in a colander and scald with boiling water. Transfer to a large saucepan and pour in the coconut milk. Bring to the boil over moderate heat. Lower the heat, cover the pan and simmer for 45 minutes, until tender.

2 Add the thyme, seasoning pepper, spring onions, garlic, salt and black pepper.

3 Wash the rice, drain and add to the beans. Add 300ml/½ pint cold water and bring to the boil over moderate heat. Lower the heat, cover the pan and simmer for 20 minutes, or until the rice is tender and all the liquid has been absorbed.

4 Remove the seasoning pepper and mix the rice and beans together with a fork. Transfer to a warmed serving dish and serve immediately.

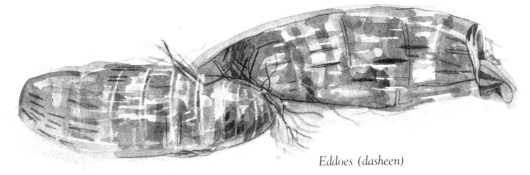

Eddoes (dasheen)

Creole Rice

The hot seasoning pepper gives Creole Rice a characteristic Caribbean flavour.

2 tablespoons olive oil
1 onion, finely chopped
2 garlic cloves, crushed
225g/8oz rice, rinsed and drained
1 hot seasoning pepper
salt and freshly ground black pepper
2 tablespoons finely chopped fresh parsley
1 red pepper, seeded and finely sliced

Serves 4

1 Heat the oil in a saucepan over moderate heat. Add the onion and cook for 5 minutes. Lower the heat, add the garlic and cook for 1 minute.

2 Stir in the rice and cook for 1 minute. Pour in 600ml/1 pint of boiling water, and add the seasoning pepper. Cover the pan and cook for 15-20 minutes, until the rice is tender and the water is absorbed.

3 Remove the seasoning pepper and season to taste with salt and black pepper.

4 Transfer to a warmed serving dish. Sprinkle over the parsley and the sliced red pepper and serve the rice immediately.

Curried Green Bananas

Curried Green Bananas will add spice to any meal. Serve as a vegetable accompaniment to any of these Caribbean dishes or as part of an Indian meal. If a sweeter flavour is preferred use slightly riper bananas and reduce the cooking time.

2 tablespoons oil
1 onion, finely sliced
1 tablespoon garam masala
4 green bananas, peeled and cut into 2.5cm/1in slices
400ml/14fl oz coconut milk (see page 16)
salt and freshly ground black pepper
1 tablespoon finely chopped fresh coriander, to garnish

Serves 4

1 Heat the oil in a saucepan, add the onion and fry over moderate heat for 6 minutes until light brown.

2 Add the garam masala to the pan and cook, stirring constantly for 1 minute.

3 Add the green bananas and cook for a further 5 minutes, until lightly browned.

4 Pour over the coconut milk. Season to taste with salt and black pepper and bring to the boil. Lower the heat, cover the pan and simmer for 30 minutes.

5 Transfer to a warmed serving dish, garnish with the chopped coriander and serve immediately.

Stuffed Sweet Potato Balls

These unusual potato balls are so delicious they could be eaten just by themselves. They are crispy on the outside with a centre filling of sweet potato, melted cheese and olives.

1kg/2lb 3oz sweet potatoes, peeled and cut into cubes
2 teaspoons salt
50g/2oz butter
2 eggs, beaten
freshly ground black pepper
100g/4oz Mozzarella or Edam cheese, cut into 18 cubes
18 stuffed olives
150g/6oz dry breadcrumbs
oil, for deep-frying
parsley sprigs, to garnish

Makes 18

1 Put the sweet potatoes into a large saucepan. Pour over enough cold water to cover. Add 1 teaspoon of the salt and bring to the boil over moderate heat. Cover and cook for 15 minutes, until soft.

2 Remove from the heat, drain and return to the pan. Add the butter, the remaining salt, half the beaten egg and black pepper to taste. Using a potato masher, mash to a smooth purée.

3 Form the purée into eighteen 5cm/2in balls. Push a piece of cheese and an olive into the centre of each ball and re-form the potato around them.

4 Sprinkle the breadcrumbs on to one large plate, and pour the remaining beaten egg into a bowl. Roll the potato balls, first in the egg then in the breadcrumbs until well coated.

5 Heat about 7.5cm/3in of oil in a saucepan. When hot, add the potato balls and fry, a few at a time, for 2-2½ minutes until golden brown. Using a slotted spoon transfer the fried potato balls to absorbent paper to drain. Keep warm while frying the remaining potato balls.

7 Transfer to a warmed serving dish, garnish with the parsley sprigs and serve immediately.

Okra in Spicy Tomato Sauce

A delicious dish for those who enjoy garlic and chilli. Okra in Spicy Tomato Sauce is the perfect accompaniment to plain meat or fish.

450g/1lb okra, trimmed

For the sauce
2 tablespoons olive oil
1 large Spanish onion, finely chopped
4 garlic cloves, crushed
6 large tomatoes, skinned and chopped
1 fresh chilli, finely chopped
1 tablespoon finely chopped fresh basil
⅛ teaspoon curry powder
1 teaspoon salt
freshly ground black pepper
snipped basil leaves, to garnish

Serves 4

1 Make the sauce: heat the oil in a large saucepan. Add the onion and fry over moderate heat for 5 minutes until soft and golden.

2 Add the garlic and fry for a further 2 minutes, stirring constantly.

3 Stir in the tomatoes, chilli, basil, curry powder, salt and pepper, and pour over 175ml/6fl oz water. Bring to the boil, then reduce the heat and simmer for 5 minutes.

4 Add the prepared okra to the pan and cook for 15-20 minutes, depending on the size of the okra, stirring occasionally.

5 Taste and adjust the seasoning. Transfer to a warmed serving dish, garnish with basil leaves and serve immediately.

Okra in Spicy Tomato Sauce (front) and
Stuffed Sweet Potato Balls

Black-Eyed Bean Fritters
Akkra

Black-Eyed Bean Fritters, which originally came from West Africa, are found throughout the Caribbean. In Jamaica they are called Akkra and in the Dutch islands, Calas.

225g/8oz black-eyed beans
1 green pepper, seeded and finely chopped
½ teaspoon Hot Pepper Sauce (see page 95)
salt and freshly ground black pepper
225ml/8fl oz oil

Makes 36

1 Put the beans in a bowl and pour over boiling water to cover. Leave to soak overnight. Drain and refresh under cold water then rub the skins off the beans with your fingers or between a tea towel.

2 Put the skinned beans and the chopped pepper into a blender or food processor and process until they form a smooth purée, adding a little water if necessary. Alternatively pound in a mortar.

3 Add the pepper sauce to the purée and season to taste with salt and black pepper.

4 Heat the oil in a heavy-based frying-pan. Drop tablespoons of the purée, a few at a time, into the oil and fry for 2-3 minutes, until golden brown, turning once. Remove with a slotted spoon and transfer to absorbent paper to drain while making the remaining fritters.

5 Arrange the fritters on a warmed serving dish and serve immediately.

Plantain Balls
Foo Foo

Serve these pounded green Plantain Balls, or Foo Foo, with soups or stews as a rather unusual substitute for dumplings.

2 green plantains
salt and freshly ground black pepper

Makes 12

1 Put the unpeeled plantains into a large saucepan. Pour in enough cold water to cover and bring to the boil over moderate heat. Lower the heat and simmer the plantains for 30 minutes until soft and the skin has begun to split.

2 Drain the plantains and when cool enough to handle, peel and place in a mortar. Season to taste with salt and black pepper.

3 Pound the plantains with a pestle for 25-30 minutes or until they form a smooth ball, dipping the pestle into cold water from time to time to prevent it from sticking.

4 Wetting your hands, roll the plantains into small balls and add to soups or stews as a garnish.

Cornmeal and Okra Pudding
Coo Coo

Cornmeal and Okra Pudding is found throughout the Caribbean. In Barbados it is called Coo Coo, in the Dutch and Virgin islands it is called Fungi or Funchi. It is served as a starchy vegetable to accompany either meat or fish.

175g/6oz okra, trimmed and sliced
1½ teaspoons salt
350g/12oz coarse cornmeal
50g/2oz butter

For the garnish
½ red pepper, seeded and diced
½ green pepper, seeded and diced

Serves 6-8

1 Put the okra into a medium saucepan. Add 900ml/1½ pints cold water and the salt and bring to the boil over moderate heat. Lower the heat, cover the pan and simmer for 10 minutes.

2 Using a wooden spoon, gradually stir in the cornmeal a little at a time. Continue cooking, stirring constantly, for 5 minutes, until the mixture comes away from the sides and bottom of the pan and forms a solid ball.

3 Using half the butter, grease a round serving dish. Spoon in the cornmeal, smoothing the top flat. Spread the remaining butter over the top.

4 Garnish with the diced peppers and serve at once.

Sweetcorn Pie

A favourite family dish, Sweetcorn Pie is the perfect accompaniment to Pineapple Spare Ribs (see page 61).

2 tablespoons oil
1 onion, finely chopped
2 × 300g/11oz cans creamed sweetcorn
2 eggs, beaten
2 teaspoons Worcestershire sauce
⅛ teaspoon paprika
salt and freshly ground black pepper

Serves 4

1 Heat the oven to 180C/350F/Gas. 4.

2 Heat the oil in a small frying-pan. Add the onion and fry over moderate heat for 5 minutes.

3 Transfer the onion to an ovenproof serving dish. Stir in the sweetcorn, eggs, Worcestershire sauce and paprika. Season to taste with salt and black pepper.

4 Bake in the oven for 45 minutes until firm and golden brown on the top. Serve immediately.

Sunshine Salad

Serve this attractive bitter-sweet salad as part of a buffet meal or as a refreshing accompaniment to most poultry or meat dishes.

4 oranges, peeled and sliced
2 large firm ripe mangoes, peeled and sliced
3 large heads of chicory, washed, dried
and leaves separated
1 tablespoon finely chopped fresh chives, to garnish

For the dressing
1 teaspoon prepared mustard
1 teaspoon sugar
2 garlic cloves, crushed
2 tablespoons finely chopped fresh chives
½ teaspoon grated orange rind
2 tablespoons fresh orange juice
2 tablespoons fresh lime juice
6 tablespoons olive oil
salt and freshly ground black pepper

Serves 4-6

1 Make the dressing: mix the mustard, sugar, garlic and chives together in a mixing bowl. Stir in the orange rind, orange juice and lime juice and gradually whisk in the oil. Season to taste with salt and freshly ground black pepper.

2 Arrange the oranges, mangoes and chicory on a plate in the shape of a sunburst. Pour over the dressing, sprinkle over the chives and serve immediately.

Bean Salad

Bean Salad improves with keeping and should be made at least one day before you wish to serve it.

100g/4oz dried red kidney beans, soaked overnight
and drained
100g/4oz dried cannellini beans, soaked overnight
and drained
1 large onion, thinly sliced
2 spring onions, trimmed and finely chopped
100g/4oz cauliflower florets
2 celery stalks, chopped
½ green pepper, seeded and thinly sliced
½ red pepper, seeded and thinly sliced
3 tablespoons finely chopped fresh parsley

For the dressing
2 teaspoons salt
50g/2oz brown sugar
150ml/¼ pint malt vinegar

Serves 6

1 Put the drained beans in a large saucepan. Cover with cold water and bring to the boil over moderate heat. Boil for 10 minutes, skimming off any scum that rises to the surface. Lower the heat and simmer for 1-1½ hours, or until the beans are tender. Drain, refresh under cold water and transfer to a large mixing bowl. Set aside to cool.

2 Add the onion, spring onions, cauliflower, celery, green and red pepper and parsley to the beans.

3 Make the dressing: put the salt, sugar, vinegar and 50ml/2fl oz of water into a small saucepan. Bring to the boil over moderate heat and continue boiling for about 30 seconds. Remove from the heat and set aside to cool.

4 Pour the cooled dressing over the vegetables and mix well. Cover with cling film and refrigerate for at least 4 hours or overnight, stirring occasionally.

5 Transfer the salad to a serving bowl and serve at room temperature.

On previous page, clockwise from the left: Bean Salad, Tropical Spinach Salad, Sunshine Salad and Yam Salad

Tropical Spinach Salad

Use young tender spinach leaves for this salad. An interesting combination of spinach, pawpaw, bacon and cashew nuts provides a delicate balance of sweet and savoury flavours. Additional bacon can be used to make a slightly more substantial salad which can be served with crusty French bread as a light lunchtime meal.

175g/6oz streaky bacon
350g/12oz fresh young spinach
1 pawpaw peeled, quartered, seeded and thinly sliced
100g/4oz cashew nuts, toasted

For the dressing
1 teaspoon prepared mustard
2 garlic cloves, crushed
3 tablespoons white wine vinegar
6 tablespoons olive oil
salt and freshly ground black pepper

Serves 4-6

1 Make the dressing: mix the mustard and garlic together in a mixing bowl. Stir in the vinegar and gradually whisk in the oil. Season to taste with salt and black pepper.

2 Heat the grill to high and grill the bacon for 5-7 minutes on each side until crispy. Set aside to cool. When cool cut up into small pieces.

3 Rinse the spinach under cold water and dry thoroughly. Pull the leaves from the stems. Discard the stems and place the leaves in a salad bowl. Add the pawpaw, nuts and bacon.

4 Just before serving pour over the dressing and toss the salad.

Yam Salad

One of the staple foods of the Caribbean, yam when prepared in this way makes an imaginative alternative to potato salad.

700g/1½lb yam
2 dill pickles, finely chopped
2 hard-boiled eggs, chopped
2 tomatoes, diced
3 spring onions, trimmed and finely chopped
2 celery stalks, diced
1 tablespoon finely chopped fresh chives
1 teaspoon salt
freshly ground black pepper
1 teaspoon paprika

For the dressing
125ml/4fl oz mayonnaise
3 tablespoons natural yoghurt
2 tablespoons cider vinegar

Serves 6-8

1 Make the dressing: mix the mayonnaise, yoghurt and cider vinegar together in a small bowl. Set aside.

2 Put the unpeeled yam in a large saucepan. Cover with water and bring to the boil. Cook for 20-25 minutes, until tender when tested with a knife.

3 Drain and when just cool enough to handle, peel and chop the yam into 1.5cm/½in cubes.

4 Put the warm yam into a large mixing bowl and pour over the dressing, mixing well to ensure the yam is thoroughly coated.

5 Add the pickles, eggs, tomatoes, spring onions, celery, chives, salt, pepper and paprika and mix well.

6 Transfer to a serving bowl. Cover with cling film and chill in the refrigerator for 1 hour. Mix well before serving.

Avocado and Pink Grapefruit Salad

Avocado and grapefruit are a favourite combination in the Caribbean where avocados, also called zabocas or alligator pears, can weigh up to several pounds each. They have smooth shiny skins and yellow buttery flesh.

2 pink grapefruits
2 large firm ripe avocado pears

For the dressing
1 teaspoon sugar
1 teaspoon French mustard
1 large garlic clove, crushed
4 tablespoons fresh grapefruit juice
5 tablespoons olive oil
salt and freshly ground black pepper

Serves 4

1 Make the dressing: mix the sugar, mustard and garlic together in a bowl. Pour over the grapefruit juice and mix well. Gradually pour in the oil, beating the mixture with a hand whisk. Season to taste with salt and pepper.

2 Peel the grapefruit and separate into segments, discarding the pips and membrane.

3 Peel and thinly slice the avocados, lengthways.

4 Arrange the avocados and grapefruits on a large round serving dish. Pour over the dressing and serve the salad immediately.

Soused Green Bananas

Green bananas are used a great deal in West Indian cooking as a starchy vegetable. They are also known locally as green figs. Soused Green Bananas tastes even better if made a few days before serving.

5 green bananas
1 cucumber, thinly sliced

For the dressing
1 tablespoon salt
1 large onion, finely chopped
juice of 2 limes
freshly ground black pepper

Serves 6-8

1 Put the unpeeled green bananas in a large saucepan, cover with cold water and bring to the boil over moderate heat. Lower the heat and simmer for 30 minutes, or until the skins of the bananas split.

2 Drain and when cool enough to handle, peel and scrape the bananas and slice into 2.5cm/1in lengths.

3 Put the sliced bananas into a heatproof bowl. Pour over enough boiling water to cover. Add the salt, onion, lime juice and black pepper to taste.

4 When cool, cover the bowl with cling film and refrigerate overnight.

5 Add the cucumber slices and serve immediately.

Avocado and Pink Grapefruit Salad (front) and
Soused Green Bananas

Caribbean Coleslaw

A sweet coleslaw salad which should be served with a salty meat such as ham or salt beef.

½ small white cabbage, finely shredded
4 large carrots, finely grated
400g/14oz can pineapple cubes, drained

For the mayonnaise
4 tablespoons condensed milk
1 tablespoon prepared mustard
1 teaspoon salt
8 tablespoons olive oil
175ml/6fl oz evaporated milk
3 tablespoons white wine vinegar
freshly ground black pepper

Serves 6

1 Make the mayonnaise: mix the condensed milk mustard and salt together in a bowl. Using an electric beater gradually add the oil, a drop at a time, whisking constantly until the mixture has thickened. Then continue to add the oil in a thin stream, whisking constantly. Gradually beat in the evaporated milk then the vinegar and black pepper. Taste and add more salt if necessary.

2 Mix the cabbage, carrot and pineapple cubes together in a large mixing bowl. Pour over the mayonnaise and toss well, ensuring all the ingredients are thoroughly coated.

3 Transfer to a glass serving bowl. Cover with cling film and chill in the refrigerator until ready to serve.

Carrot and Sultana Salad

The cinnamon in this salad gives it a distinctive and unusual flavour. A good tip for crisping up carrots is to soak them in iced water for 1 hour before you grate them.

450g/1lb carrots, peeled and grated
100g/4oz sultanas
juice of ½ orange
juice of ½ lime
4 tablespoons mayonnaise
1¼ teaspoons ground cinnamon
½ teaspoon salt
freshly ground black pepper

Serves 4

1 Put the carrots and sultanas into a mixing bowl. Pour over the orange and lime juice and mix well.

2 Gradually stir in the mayonnaise. Add 1 teaspoon of the cinnamon, the salt and black pepper and mix well together, ensuring that all the ingredients are thoroughly combined.

3 Spoon into a serving bowl, sprinkle over the remaining cinnamon and serve at once.

Rice and Pepper Salad with Tomato Dressing

This tangy rice salad flavoured with tomatoes, peppers and garlic is delicious served with any meat, fish or poultry dish. It is very important to rinse the rice thoroughly before cooking to prevent it from becoming sticky.

2 tablespoons olive oil
1 onion, finely chopped
2 garlic cloves, crushed
1 red pepper, seeded and diced
1 green pepper, seeded and diced
225g/8oz rice, rinsed and drained
1 hot seasoning pepper
salt and freshly ground black pepper

For the dressing
5 tomatoes, skinned, seeded and chopped
1 garlic clove
2 tablespoons red wine vinegar
6 tablespoons olive oil
1 teaspoon dried thyme

To garnish
tomato slices
fresh thyme sprigs

Serves 4-6

1 Make the dressing: put the chopped tomatoes, garlic, wine vinegar, olive oil, thyme, and salt and pepper together in an electric blender or food processor and process for 30-60 seconds, or until it is smooth and fairly thick.

2 Heat the oil in a saucepan over moderate heat. Add the onion and cook for 5 minutes until softened. Lower the heat, add the garlic, red and green peppers and cook for 2 minutes.

3 Stir in the rice and cook for 1 minute. Pour in 600ml/1 pint of boiling water and add the seasoning pepper. Cover the pan and cook for 15-20 minutes, until the rice is tender and the water is absorbed.

4 Remove the seasoning pepper and season to taste with salt and pepper.

5 Transfer to a serving dish and pour over the tomato dressing. Mix well together and set aside to cool.

6 Garnish with the tomato slices and thyme sprigs before serving.

Cucumber and Coconut Salad

Spicy and refreshing, Cucumber and Coconut Salad reflects the East Indian influence that is present in Caribbean cooking.

1 cucumber, seeded and cut into 1.5cm/½in cubes
3 tablespoons desiccated coconut

For the dressing
2 teaspoons sugar
4 tablespoons fresh lime or lemon juice
½ teaspoon seeded and finely chopped fresh chilli
salt and white pepper

Serves 4

1 Make the dressing: mix the sugar with the lime or lemon juice in a small bowl. Add the chilli, season with salt and white pepper to taste and mix well.

2 Put the cucumber into a serving bowl, pour over the dressing and mix well, ensuring the pieces are thoroughly coated. Sprinkle over the coconut and serve immediately.

Hot Pepper Sauce

Each island in the Caribbean has its own recipe for Hot Pepper Sauce. It is served as a condiment with most meals and when used with discretion can become quite addictive.

*225g/8oz red, green and yellow hot seasoning peppers,
seeded and finely chopped
2 large onions, finely chopped
2 garlic cloves, finely chopped
½ small unripe pawpaw, skinned, seeded
and finely chopped
2 teaspoons Dijon mustard
½ teaspoon turmeric
1 teaspoon salt
625ml/21fl oz white distilled vinegar*

Makes 1.1l/2 pints

1 Put the peppers, onions, garlic, pawpaw, mustard, turmeric, salt and vinegar into a saucepan. Bring to the boil over moderate heat. Lower the heat and simmer for 5 minutes.

2 Pour into warmed sterilized jars, cover with a circle of greaseproof paper and seal with airtight, vinegar-proof lids. The sauce will keep for several months.

Pepper Wine

A few drops of Pepper Wine transform a simple soup or stew into an exotic West Indian dish.

*3 hot seasoning peppers
1 bottle dry sherry*

1 Put the peppers into a large glass preserving jar, pour over the sherry and leave for 2 weeks. (Keep the sherry bottle.)

2 Using a funnel, pour the sherry back into the bottle adding one of the peppers, and use as required.

From the left: Pepper Jelly, Sweet Pepper Sauce (on shelf) and Garlic and Pepper Sauce, Hot Pepper Sauce, Spicy Mustard Pickle, Pepper Wine

Sweet Pepper Sauce

Sweet Pepper Sauce is an adaptation of a traditional pepper and tomato sauce served with black beans in Cuba. Serve this spicy sauce with beans, meat, fish or rice.

175ml/6fl oz olive oil
700g/1½lb tomatoes, skinned and chopped
450g/1lb red peppers, seeded and very finely chopped
1 bay leaf
1 fresh red chilli, seeded and finely chopped
3 garlic cloves, crushed
1 teaspoon dried oregano
1 tablespoon finely chopped fresh coriander
1 teaspoon sugar
salt and freshly ground black pepper
4 tablespoons white wine vinegar

Makes about 1.1l/2 pints

1 Heat the oil in a saucepan, add the tomatoes, red peppers and bay leaf and cook over moderate heat for 10 minutes, stirring constantly.

2 Add the chilli, garlic, oregano, coriander and sugar. Season to taste with salt and black pepper. Lower the heat and cook for a further 15 minutes, stirring frequently, until the sauce is thick. Remove from the heat and pour in the vinegar.

3 Pour into warmed sterilized jars and seal with airtight vinegar-proof lids. The sauce will keep for several months.

Spicy Mustard Pickle
Chow Chow

Spicy Mustard Pickle will keep for several months in an airtight jar. Serve Chow Chow with cold meats and salad.

½ small cauliflower, separated into small florets
2 green tomatoes, chopped
2 onions, chopped
3 carrots, chopped
10 green beans, trimmed and chopped
1 fresh chilli, seeded and chopped
2 tablespoons salt
350ml/12fl oz white wine vinegar
2 tablespoons cornflour
2 tablespoons sugar
1 tablespoon mustard powder
1 teaspoon curry powder
1 teaspoon turmeric

Makes 1.1l/2 pints

1 Put the cauliflower, tomatoes, onions, carrots, beans and chilli into a large mixing bowl. Pour over 900ml/1½ pints cold water and stir in the salt. Cover the bowl and leave overnight.

2 Drain the vegetables and transfer to a saucepan. Pour in 300ml/½ pint cold water, add 2 tablespoons of the vinegar and bring to the boil over moderate heat. Lower the heat and simmer for 5 minutes.

3 Meanwhile mix the cornflour, sugar, mustard, curry powder and turmeric together in a bowl. Stir in the remaining vinegar to form a smooth paste. Mix a little of the hot cooking water into the paste then pour the paste into the pan. Simmer for 2 minutes then remove from the heat.

4 Transfer to warmed sterilized jars and seal with screw-top vinegar-proof lids.

Garlic and Pepper Sauce

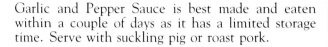

Garlic and Pepper Sauce is best made and eaten within a couple of days as it has a limited storage time. Serve with suckling pig or roast pork.

2 hot seasoning peppers, seeded and chopped
2 green peppers, seeded and chopped
6 garlic cloves
2 tablespoons finely chopped fresh parsley
juice of 2 limes
125ml/4fl oz olive oil
1 teaspoon salt
freshly ground black pepper

Makes about 450ml/16fl oz

1 Put the seasoning peppers, green peppers, garlic and parsley into a food processor or blender and process for 30 seconds until they form a smooth purée.

2 Pour in the lime juice, olive oil, salt and black pepper and process for a further 15 seconds until thoroughly blended. Pour into sterilized jars and seal with airtight lids. Store in the refrigerator.

Pepper Jelly

Pepper Jelly is slightly hot and very sweet. It is delicious served with any roast meat.

1kg/2lb 3oz cooking apples, chopped
150ml/¼ pint cider vinegar
450g/1lb sugar
2 hot seasoning peppers

Makes about 700g/1½lb

1 Put the apples in a large heavy-based saucepan together with the vinegar and 450ml/¾ pint of water. Bring to the boil, then lower the heat slightly and simmer for 20-25 minutes, or until the apples are very soft and pulpy.

2 Hang a jelly bag over a large bowl and pour the apple pulp into the bag. Leave the pulp to strain through overnight.

3 Transfer the strained juice to a large pan, add the sugar and 1 seasoning pepper and heat gently, stirring constantly, until the sugar has dissolved. Bring to the boil, then continue to boil vigorously for about 5 minutes until a teaspoon of the jelly placed on a cold saucer wrinkles when a finger is pulled across the surface. Discard the seasoning pepper.

4 Remove the pan from the heat and skim off any scum. Seed and finely chop the remaining seasoning pepper, then stir into the jelly. Pour the jelly immediately into warmed sterilized 225g/8oz jam jars. Place a circle of greaseproof paper on the surface of the jelly and when cool, seal the jars with airtight lids. Store for up to 9 months.

DESSERTS

Caribbean desserts tend to be either very sweet, very fruity or very alcoholic, usually a mixture of all three. Because dairy products such as fresh cream are unavailable on most of the islands, those who live there have to rely on canned cream, evaporated and condensed milk. But the recipes in this section, where possible, have been adapted to use fresh cream. Coconut is also used a great deal as the basis for many of their delicious desserts. In my opinion though, it is the tropical fruits with their exotic flavours and colours (see Tropical Fruit Platter, page 105) that provide the best ending to any Caribbean meal.

Mango and Coconut Meringue

The best way to eat a mango is sitting in the bath! The second best way is to eat it in a dessert like Mango and Coconut Meringue. The meringue can be made the day before and should be filled just before serving.

4 egg whites
pinch of salt
225g/8oz caster sugar
1 teaspoon cornflour
1 teaspoon white wine vinegar
3 tablespoons desiccated coconut
3 bay leaves, to decorate

For the filling
2 large firm ripe mangoes, peeled and sliced
450ml/¾ pint double cream
2 tablespoons caster sugar
1 egg white

Serves 6-8

1 Heat the oven to 140C/275F/Gas 1.

2 Using an electric beater, whisk the egg whites and a pinch of salt until stiff. Gradually beat in the caster sugar, then continue beating for 5 minutes.

3 Fold the cornflour, vinegar and coconut into the meringue mixture. Line a baking sheet with silicone paper. Using a palette knife, shape the meringue in a 23cm/9in circle on the baking sheet, building up the edges to form a ridge.

4 Bake in the centre of the oven for 10 minutes, then lower the oven to 110C/225F/Gas ¼ and cook for a further 45 minutes. Turn off the oven and leave the meringue in the cooling oven for 1 hour. Remove and transfer to a large flat serving plate.

5 Make the filling: put one of the sliced mangoes in a food processor or blender and process for 30 seconds, until it forms a smooth purée. Transfer to a bowl and set aside.

6 Using an electric beater, gently whisk the cream and sugar together until it is thick and firm. Whisk the egg white in another bowl until it is stiff, then fold into the cream with the mango purée.

7 Fill the centre of the meringue with the cream and mango mixture. Decorate the top with the remaining mango slices and bay leaves and serve.

Mango and Coconut Meringue (front) and
Lime Bombe with Mango Sauce

Lime Bombe with Mango Sauce

Lime Bombe with Mango Sauce is an impressive dessert to serve at an elegant dinner party. If limes are unavailable lemons may be used instead.

finely grated rind of 3 limes
juice of 4 limes
3 eggs, separated
pinch of salt
100g/4oz caster sugar
300ml/½ pint double cream

For the mango sauce
425g/15oz can mangoes
juice of 1 lime

To decorate
cubes of mango
shreds of lime rind

Serves 6-8

1 Mix the lime rind and juice together in a bowl.

2 Using an electric beater, whisk the egg whites and a pinch of salt until stiff. Gradually beat in 75g/3oz of the sugar. Beat the egg yolks into the mixture.

3 In a separate bowl, whisk the cream with the remaining sugar, then add the mixed lime rind and juice and whisk until firm.

4 Using a metal spoon, fold the lime mixture into the egg mixture. Pour into a 900ml/1½ pint pudding basin, cover with cling film and freeze overnight.

5 Make the sauce: put the mangoes and their juice with the lime juice into a blender or food processor and process for 30 seconds, until they form a smooth purée. Strain into a small jug.

6 Unmould the bombe 2 hours before serving: dip the bottom of the bowl into a basin of cold water, run a knife around the inside edge and turn out on to a serving dish. Return to the freezer.

7 About 15 minutes before serving, remove the bombe from the freezer and place in the refrigerator. Just before serving, decorate with cubes of mango and shreds of lime rind. Serve with a little of the sauce poured over the top and the rest passed separately in the jug.

Coconut Jelly

Coconut Jelly can be made with desiccated coconut instead of fresh (see page 16), and is a great favourite with children.

1 coconut
600ml/1 pint milk
1½ tablespoons powdered gelatine
3 tablespoons sugar
2 tablespoons sultanas (optional)

Serves 4-6

1 Split open the coconut and remove the flesh. Cut away the brown skin and grate the flesh. Transfer to a bowl.

2 Scald the milk and pour over the grated coconut. Leave for 30 minutes, stirring frequently. Strain the milk into a saucepan, squeezing the coconut with your hands to extract all the liquid.

3 Mix the gelatine with 3 tablespoons of the coconut milk in a small ramekin dish, and pour the mixture into the saucepan.

4 Add the sugar, place the pan over low heat and cook for 3 minutes, stirring constantly. Do not allow to boil. Stir in the sultanas, if using, and pour into a 600ml/1 pint jelly mould. Set aside to cool.

5 When cool, place in the refrigerator for 2-3 hours until set.

6 Unmould and serve immediately.

Creole Crêpes

Creole Crêpes are delicious by themselves, or try them filled with Coconut Ice Cream (see page 109).

40g/1½oz butter, melted

For the batter
225g/8oz plain flour
pinch of salt
2 eggs
450ml/¾ pint milk
150ml/¼ pint coconut milk (see page 16)
2 tablespoons brandy or rum
2 tablespoons brown sugar
50g/2oz butter, melted
½ teaspoon ground cinnamon
⅛ teaspoon ground cloves
⅛ teaspoon grated nutmeg

For the sauce
5 tablespoons brandy
6 tablespoons granulated sugar
2 teaspoons ground cinnamon

Makes 12

1 Make the crêpe batter: sift the flour and salt together into a large mixing bowl. Make a well in the centre and gradually beat in the eggs, milk and coconut milk until the mixture forms a smooth batter.

2 Stir in the brandy, sugar, butter, cinnamon, cloves and nutmeg.

3 Heat a 20cm/8in frying-pan. Brush with a little melted butter and pour in about 2 tablespoons of the batter, enough to thinly coat the bottom of the pan. Tip the pan as you pour, so that the bottom is evenly coated.

4 Cook for 30 seconds then turn the crêpe over and cook for a further 30 seconds until golden brown. Remove with a spatula, roll up the crêpe and place in an ovenproof serving dish. Keep warm in a very low oven while you fry the remaining crêpes.

5 Make the sauce: put the brandy, sugar and cinnamon in a small saucepan. Place over low heat and cook for 2 minutes, until the sugar has melted. Remove from the heat, pour over the crêpes and serve immediately.

Rum and Banana Mousse

Bananas and rum are two ingredients which feature strongly in Caribbean cooking. And the two combine deliciously in this rich, alcoholic dessert.

2 tablespoons powdered gelatine
175ml/6fl oz rum
3 ripe bananas, mashed
2 teaspoons vanilla essence
5 eggs, separated
pinch of salt
75g/3oz caster sugar
450ml/¾ pint double cream
⅛ teaspoon grated nutmeg

Serves 6

1 Sprinkle the gelatine over 4 tablespoons of the rum in a small ramekin dish. Leave to soak for 5 minutes, then put the ramekin into a small saucepan of gently simmering water and heat gently for 2-3 minutes, until the gelatine has completely dissolved, stirring occasionally. Remove from the heat and set aside to cool.

2 Put the bananas, the remaining rum and vanilla essence into a food processor or blender and process for 1 minute, or until they form a smooth purée. Set the banana mixture aside.

3 Using an electric beater, whisk the egg whites and a pinch of salt until stiff. Gradually add half the sugar, whisking constantly.

4 Whisk the remaining sugar with the egg yolks until light and fluffy. Beat in 300ml/½ pint of the cream and continue beating for 5 minutes.

5 Add the banana mixture to the cream mixture, then fold in the egg whites and the gelatine.

6 Pour the mousse into a decorative glass bowl. Cover with cling film and refrigerate for 2-3 hours or until set.

7 Whisk the remaining cream in a bowl until firm. Remove the mousse from the refrigerator and pipe the cream on top in rosettes, sprinkle over the nutmeg and serve immediately.

Lime Meringue Pie

Lime Meringue Pie can be found in most of the Caribbean islands. A popular dessert, it is the perfect combination of sweet crisp meringue with tangy scented limes.

For the pastry
75g/3oz plain flour
pinch of salt
1/4 teaspoon baking powder
2 teaspoons sugar
40g/1 1/2oz butter

For the filling
175g/6oz sugar
grated rind and juice of 5 limes
2 tablespoons plain flour
4 tablespoons cornflour
3 egg yolks

For the meringue
3 egg whites
pinch of salt
175g/6oz caster sugar

Serves 6

1 Make the pastry: sift the flour, salt and baking powder into a mixing bowl. Add the sugar, then rub in the butter until the mixture resembles fine breadcrumbs. Using a knife, mix in 1 1/2 tablespoons of cold water until a stiff but non-sticky dough is formed. Knead lightly on a floured surface until smooth. Roll out and line a 20cm/8in pie dish. Chill in the refrigerator for 20 minutes.

2 Pre-heat the oven to 200C/400F/Gas 6 and bake the pastry shell 'blind' for 10-15 minutes or until it is lightly browned. Set aside to cool.

3 Make the filling: dissolve the sugar with 400ml/14fl oz of hot water in a medium saucepan over low heat. Add the lime rind and juice.

4 Mix the flour and cornflour with 3 tablespoons of cold water in a small bowl to form a smooth paste.

5 Stir the paste into the lime and sugar and bring to the boil over a moderate heat, stirring constantly. Boil vigorously for 2 minutes then remove from the heat and set aside to cool.

6 Add the egg yolks to the pan and place over a low heat. Bring the mixture to simmering point, stirring constantly, but do not allow it to boil.

7 Remove from the heat and pour into the prepared pastry case. Set aside to cool and set.

8 Heat the oven to 180C/350F/Gas 4.

9 Make the meringue: using an electric beater, whisk the egg whites and salt until stiff. Add the sugar *very* gradually, whisking the mixture constantly until stiff peaks are formed.

10 Spread the mixture on top of the pie and bake in the centre of the oven for 10-15 minutes or until the meringue is lightly browned.

11 Remove from the oven and serve hot or cold.

Lime Meringue Pie

Bananas Flambés

A simple dessert from Martinique which never fails to impress as it is brought still flaming to the table.

6 large bananas
grated rind of ½ orange
juice of 1 orange
⅛ teaspoon grated nutmeg
4 tablespoons sugar
50g/2oz butter, plus 1 tablespoon, for greasing
125ml/4fl oz rum

Serves 6

1 Heat the oven to 180C/350F/Gas 4. Grease a shallow ovenproof serving dish with the tablespoon of butter.

2 Put the unpeeled bananas on a baking sheet and bake in the centre of the oven for 10 minutes, turning once, until they have turned black.

3 Remove from the oven and when cool enough to handle, peel off the skins and arrange the bananas in the serving dish.

4 Heat the grill to high.

5 Mix the orange rind, orange juice and nutmeg together in a small bowl and pour over the bananas. Sprinkle over the sugar and dot surface with the remaining butter.

6 Place the bananas under the grill for 6-8 minutes, or until the sugar is bubbling.

7 Meanwhile put the rum into a small saucepan and heat gently over low heat for 2 minutes.

8 Remove the bananas from the grill. Ignite the rum in the saucepan with a match and pour the flaming rum over the bananas. Serve immediately while rum is still flaming.

Pink Grapefruit Bowl

In the Caribbean this dessert would be made with a sharp-tasting red-fleshed citrus fruit called shaddock or pomelo. The slightly sweeter grapefruit is believed to have developed from this fruit, which was first introduced to the Caribbean from Polynesia in the 17th century.

6 pink grapefruits
4 tablespoons rum
dash of Angostura bitters
225g/8oz caster sugar

Serves 4-6

1 Thinly pare the peel from one of the grapefruits, using a fruit parer. Cut into matchsticks and reserve. Peel the grapefruits: using a very sharp knife cut off a slice from both ends of the fruit. Then cut off the skin downwards, taking the pith with it. Cut out each segment from between the pithy membrane.

2 Put the segments into a large heatproof serving bowl. Pour in the rum and a dash of the bitters. Mix well together.

3 Melt the sugar in a heavy-based saucepan over moderate heat for 3-5 minutes until it is a caramel colour, stirring constantly.

4 Remove from the heat and pour over the grapefruit, leaving about 1 tablespoon of caramel in the pan.

5 Pour 150ml/¼ pint boiling water into the saucepan. Add the grapefruit matchsticks and bring to the boil over moderate heat. Boil for 3 minutes. Drain and refresh under cold water.

6 Decorate the pink grapefruits with the blanched matchsticks and serve immediately.

Grapefruit Soufflé

Serve this creamy rich Grapefruit Soufflé as cold as possible, straight from the refrigerator.

175ml/6fl oz freshly squeezed pink grapefruit juice
15g/½oz powdered gelatine
175g/6oz caster sugar
4 eggs, separated
2 tablespoons finely grated grapefruit rind
pinch of salt
300ml/½ pint double cream
50g/2oz ratafia biscuits, crushed

To decorate
150ml/¼ pint double cream
8 ratafia biscuits

Serves 6-8

1 Put the grapefruit juice into a small heatproof bowl. Sprinkle over the gelatine and leave to soak for 5 minutes. Stand the bowl in a small pan of gently simmering water for 1-2 minutes until the gelatine has completely dissolved, stirring occasionally. Remove from heat, and leave to cool for 5 minutes.

2 Put the caster sugar, egg yolks and grapefruit rind into a heatproof mixing bowl. Place the bowl over a pan half-filled with simmering water and beat for 5 minutes with an electric beater, until thick and creamy. Remove from the heat and beat until cold.

3 Beat in the gelatine mixture. Cover and chill in the refrigerator for 15 minutes.

4 Using an electric beater, whisk the egg whites with a pinch of salt until stiff. Whisk the 300ml/½ pint cream in a separate bowl until firm, then fold into the egg whites.

5 Using a large metal spoon, gently fold the cream mixture into the grapefruit mixture. Pour half of the mixture into a 1.7l/3 pint soufflé dish. Cover with the crushed biscuits then gently spoon over the remaining mixture. Smooth the top with a knife and chill in the refrigerator for 3 hours, until set.

6 Whisk the 150ml/¼ pint cream until firm, then spread it over the top of the soufflé, and decorate with the whole ratafias. Serve immediately.

Tropical Fruit Platter

This spectacular dessert speaks for itself. Tropical Fruit Platter can be made with any combination of tropical fruit arranged decoratively on a platter. The delicate passion fruit syrup allows the natural flavour of the other fruit to come through.

450g/1lb watermelon, sliced, seeded and cut into wedges
1 small pineapple, halved, skinned and cut into slices,
with the top reserved
1 pawpaw, skinned and sliced
2 mangoes, skinned and sliced
2 tangerines, peeled and sliced
2 bananas, sliced

For the syrup
pulp of 6 passion fruit
2 tablespoons sugar

Serves 6-8

1 Make the syrup: put the passion fruit pulp, sugar and 125ml/4fl oz of water into a small saucepan. Bring to the boil over moderate heat and boil vigorously for 1 minute. Remove from the heat and strain the liquid through a fine mesh strainer into a jug, pushing the pulp with the back of a wooden spoon to extract all the juice. Set aside to cool.

2 Place the pineapple top in the centre of a large round glass serving dish. Arrange the fruit attractively in circles around it. Pour over the passion fruit syrup and serve immediately.

Pitch Lake Dessert Cake

This dessert cake is named after the Pitch Lake in Trinidad which provides the asphalt for constructing roads all over the world. Make it the night before and decorate with cream, chocolate and chocolate coffee beans just before serving. Use a potato peeler to pare the chocolate curls.

350g/12oz trifle sponge squares
150ml/¼ pint coffee liqueur
50ml/2fl oz milk
450ml/¾ pint double cream

For the filling
225g/8oz bitter chocolate, broken into pieces
1 tablespoon instant coffee
5 eggs, separated
pinch of salt

To decorate
50g/2oz bitter chocolate, pared into curls
chocolate coffee beans (optional)

Serves 6-8

1 Make the filling: place the chocolate, coffee and 1 tablespoon of water in a heatproof bowl and place over a pan of simmering water. Cook for 5 minutes until the chocolate and coffee have melted.

2 Remove the pan from the heat, take out the bowl and allow to cool slightly. Beat in the egg yolks, one at a time.

3 Using an electric beater, whisk the egg whites and a pinch of salt until stiff, then fold into the chocolate mixture with a metal spoon. Set aside.

4 Cut each of the sponge squares into 3 slices lengthways. Mix the coffee liqueur and the milk together in a bowl.

5 Line the bottom of a 20cm/8in loose-bottomed cake tin with greaseproof paper, then cover with a layer of the cake slices. Cut the pieces to fit, patchwork fashion. Sprinkle over one-third of the liqueur mixture, then cover with half of the mocha filling. Continue making layers in this way, ending with a layer of sponge and liqueur. Cover the top of the tin with cling film and refrigerate overnight.

6 Run a knife around the inside edge of the cake tin then unmould. Place a serving plate on top of the cake and invert the cake on to the plate. Remove the bottom of the tin and the greaseproof paper.

7 Whisk the cream until firm then, using a palette knife, completely cover the cake with the cream. Decorate the cake with chocolate curls and coffee beans, if using, and serve immediately.

Tropical Fruit Platter (front) and Pitch Lake Dessert Cake

Guava Ice Cream

Fresh guavas may be difficult to find outside the Caribbean, but canned guavas are ideal for this delicious ice cream.

2 × 425g/15oz cans guavas, drained
6 eggs
175g/6oz caster sugar
600ml/1 pint milk
1 teaspoon vanilla essence

Serves 6-8

1 Using a teaspoon, remove as many pips from the centre of the guavas as possible and discard. Pureé the remaining guava flesh in a food processor or liquidizer and set aside.

2 Lightly beat the eggs and sugar together in a medium mixing bowl. Scald the milk then pour into the egg mixture.

3 Place the bowl over a pan half-filled with simmering water. Cook, stirring constantly, for 30-35 minutes or until the custard is thick enough to coat the back of a spoon.

4 Remove from the heat and stir in the vanilla essence and guava pureé. Spoon the mixture into a china or glass dish. Leave to cool, then place in the freezer compartment and freeze for 2-3 hours or until it is just beginning to freeze.

5 Remove from the freezer and beat well, to break up the ice crystals. Return to the freezer for 3-4 hours, or overnight.

6 Remove from the freezer and place in the refrigerator 1 hour before serving, to allow the ice cream to soften slightly.

Guavas

Coconut Ice Cream

This ice cream is found throughout the Caribbean in many different styles. This recipe uses evaporated milk, producing a sweet and rich ice cream slightly reminiscent of Indian kulfi.

grated flesh of 1 coconut
6 egg yolks
100g/4oz caster sugar
450ml/¾ pint evaporated milk
1 teaspoon vanilla essence

Serves 6-8

1 Make 450ml/¾ pint coconut milk using the flesh of the coconut (see page 16).

2 Lightly beat the egg yolks and sugar together in a medium heatproof mixing bowl. Scald the evaporated milk, taking care not to let it burn. Then pour it into the egg mixture.

3 Place the bowl over a saucepan half-filled with simmering water. Cook stirring constantly for 15-20 minutes, or until the custard is thick enough to coat the back of a spoon.

4 Remove from the heat and stir in the vanilla essence and coconut milk. Spoon the mixture into a shallow china or glass dish and place in the freezer compartment and freeze for 2-3 hours or until it is just beginning to set.

5 Remove from the freezer and beat well, to break up the ice crystals. Return to the freezer for 2 hours, beat again, then freeze for a further 1-2 hours.

6 Remove from the freezer and place in the refrigerator 1 hour before serving, to allow the ice cream to soften slightly.

Ice Box Cake

Ice Box Cake is another speciality of the islands. It is very sweet, very rich and very alcoholic. The cake here will serve at least 12 and is best accompanied by strong black coffee.

450g/1lb digestive biscuits
100g/4oz butter
100g/4oz icing sugar
1 egg, beaten
350ml/12fl oz dark rum

For the icing
25g/1oz butter
1 tablespoon rum
100g/4oz icing sugar
2 tablespoons cocoa

Serves 12

1 Crumble the biscuits in a bowl until they resemble fine breadcrumbs.

2 In a medium mixing bowl cream the butter and sugar thoroughly together until the mixture becomes light and fluffy.

3 Add the beaten egg, crushed biscuits and rum and mix well.

4 Line a 1.7l/3 pint loaf tin with greaseproof paper and press the mixture into the tin. Cover with cling film and chill in the freezer for 1 hour.

5 Make the icing: melt the butter with the rum in a small saucepan over low heat. Add the icing sugar, cocoa and 3 tablespoons warm water and stir with a wooden spoon until smooth and glossy. Remove from the heat and set aside to cool to room temperature.

6 Remove the cake from the freezer and unmould on to a serving plate. Cover the top and sides with the icing, using a palette knife, and leave to set.

7 When the icing has set, cover the cake with foil and return to the freezer for at least 2 hours.

8 To serve, cut the cake into thin slices and eat while still frozen.

CAKES, BREADS AND DUMPLINGS

The best fruit cakes in the world come from the Caribbean – they are rich, moist, full of fruit and rum, almost like puddings. They are often called Black Cakes because they are packed with dark rich dried fruit. Sizzling Fruit Cake (see page 112) is my own preferred lighter version of the Black Cake and is perfect to use as a Christmas or wedding cake. The Caribbean is also famous for its delicious sweet breads, such as coconut, banana and ginger, which always prove to be great favourites with children.

Chocolate Arrowroot Cake

Arrowroot is a powdery white starch made from the young rhizomes of the *Maranta arundinacea* plant grown on the island of St Vincent. It is used extensively in Caribbean cooking as a thickening agent and for making cakes, biscuits and desserts.

100g/4oz butter, plus 1 tablespoon, for greasing
175g/6oz plain flour
50g/2oz arrowroot
50g/2oz cocoa powder
225g/8oz caster sugar
3 eggs
1 teaspoon bicarbonate of soda
2 tablespoons instant coffee granules
125ml/4fl oz milk
125ml/4fl oz soured cream
blanched tangerine peel, to decorate

For the topping
100g/4oz caster sugar
50g/2oz butter
100g/4oz plain chocolate, broken into pieces

Makes a 20cm/8in cake

1 Heat the oven to 170C/325F/Gas 3. Using 1 tablespoon of the butter grease a 20cm/8in round loose-bottomed cake tin.

2 Sift the flour, arrowroot and cocoa powder together in a bowl. Set aside.

3 Cream the butter and the sugar together in a large mixing bowl until the mixture is light and fluffy.

4 Add the eggs one at a time, beating well after each one.

5 Dissolve the bicarbonate of soda and instant coffee in the milk and add to the egg mixture, alternately with the sifted flour mixture.

6 Add the soured cream and beat well. Pour the mixture into the prepared cake tin and bake in the centre of the oven for 50-60 minutes, or until a skewer inserted into the centre comes out clean.

7 Remove from the oven and set aside to cool.

8 Make the topping: put the sugar into a saucepan with 2 tablespoons of water and stir over moderate heat until dissolved. Remove from the heat and whisk in the butter and chocolate until thick and smooth.

9 Remove the cake from the tin and spread the icing over the top. Cut the blanched tangerine peel into attractive shapes and use to decorate the cake.

Chocolate Arrowroot Cake

Sizzling Fruit Cake

Sizzling Fruit Cake acquired its name from the sound made when the rum is poured over the cake while it is still hot.

225g/8oz raisins
225g/8oz sultanas
225g/8oz currants
225g/8oz glacé cherries
225g/8oz pitted prunes
50g/2oz chopped mixed peel
700ml/1¼ pint bottle dark rum
225g/8oz butter
275g/10oz brown sugar
225g/8oz plain flour
2 teaspoons baking powder
½ teaspoon ground cloves
1 teaspoon ground cinnamon
6 eggs
4 tablespoons molasses

Makes a 23cm/9in cake

1 Mix the raisins, sultanas, currants, cherries, prunes and mixed peel together in a large bowl. Pour over 600ml/1 pint of the rum, cover with cling film and set the fruit aside to soak for 24 hours, stirring it occasionally.

2 Prepare a 23cm/9in round loose-bottomed cake tin, by lining first with brown paper then with greaseproof paper.

3 Cream the butter and sugar together until light and fluffy.

4 Sift the flour, baking powder, cloves and cinnamon together.

5 Gradually add the flour mixture to the butter and sugar, alternating with the eggs, beating well after each addition.

6 Heat the oven to 150C/300F/Gas 2.

7 Stir in the molasses then fold the mixture into the soaked fruits. Mix everything well together until thoroughly combined.

8 Spoon the mixture into the cake tin and bake in the centre of the oven for 2-2½ hours, or until a skewer inserted into the centre comes out clean.

9 Remove the cake from the oven and gently prick it all over with a fork. Pour over the remaining rum and when it has stopped sizzling, cover and cool in the tin.

10 Serve the cake sliced or, alternatively, keep it wrapped in a rum-soaked cloth then cover with a layer of marzipan and icing when required.

Banana Bread

Banana Bread is found throughout the Caribbean, each island having its own recipe. Some add sultanas, others use Brazil nuts, and some include orange zest. This particular recipe was given to me by a friend from St Kitts.

2 tablespoons margarine, plus 1 tablespoon, for greasing
150g/5oz white sugar
150g/5oz brown sugar
2 eggs, lightly beaten
350g/12oz plain flour
1 teaspoon baking powder
1 teaspoon bicarbonate of soda
½ teaspoon ground cinnamon
pinch of salt
3 large ripe bananas, mashed
4 tablespoons milk mixed with 1 teaspoon lemon juice
1 teaspoon vanilla essence
100g/4oz stoned dates, chopped
100g/4oz walnuts, chopped

Makes 2 × 450g/1lb loaves

1 Heat the oven to 150C/300F/Gas 2.

2 Grease two 450g/1lb loaf tins with the 1 tablespoon of margarine.

3 Beat the margarine, white and brown sugar, and eggs together in a bowl with an electric beater until light and creamy.

4 Sift the flour, baking powder, bicarbonate of soda, cinnamon and salt together.

5 Gradually add the sifted flour mixture to the creamed mixture, beating thoroughly after each addition of flour.

6 Stir in the bananas, milk, vanilla essence, dates and walnuts.

7 Divide the mixture between the loaf tins and bake in the centre of the oven for about 1 hour, or until a skewer inserted into the centre of the loaves comes out clean.

8 Remove from the oven, run a knife around the inside of the tins and turn the loaves out on to a wire rack to cool.

9 Serve spread with butter.

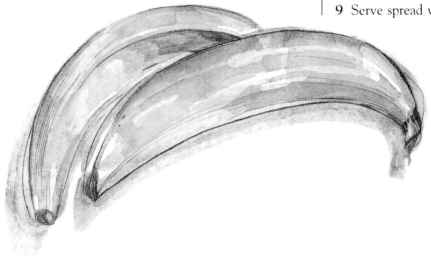

Gingerbread

A really spicy and gingery Gingerbread which can be eaten with or without butter. The longer it is kept the more moist it will become. If keeping, store in an airtight tin.

100g/4oz butter, plus 1 tablespoon, for greasing
275g/10oz plain flour
½ teaspoon salt
2 teaspoons baking powder
1 teaspoon bicarbonate of soda
2 teaspoons ground ginger
¼ teaspoon grated nutmeg
175g/6oz molasses
100g/4oz brown sugar
175ml/6fl oz milk
2 eggs, beaten
1 teaspoon grated fresh root ginger

Makes a 2lb loaf

1 Heat the oven to 170C/325F/Gas 3. Lightly grease a 900g/2lb loaf tin with the tablespoon of butter.

2 Sift the flour, salt, baking powder, bicarbonate of soda, ground ginger and nutmeg together into a large mixing bowl.

3 Melt the molasses, sugar and butter together in a small saucepan over low heat. Remove from the heat, set pan aside to cool, then add the milk and eggs, mixing well.

4 Pour into the flour and mix together thoroughly. Fold in the grated ginger. Pour the mixture into the loaf tin and cook for 50 minutes in the centre of the oven, or until a skewer inserted into the centre comes out clean.

5 Remove from the oven and cool in the tin. Turn out and serve sliced, and spread with butter if wished.

Coconut Bread

Coconut Bread is very sweet and quite dry, almost a cake rather than a bread. It can be eaten with or without butter as preferred. Desiccated coconut can be stored in a screw-top jar in the refrigerator for several weeks.

100g/4oz margarine, melted, plus 1 tablespoon, for greasing
450g/1lb plain flour
1 tablespoon baking powder
pinch of salt
225g/8oz desiccated coconut
175g/6oz caster sugar, plus 2 tablespoons, for glazing
100g/4oz raisins
1 egg, beaten
300ml/½ pint evaporated milk
1 teaspoon almond essence

Makes 2 × 450g/1lb loaves

1 Using the tablespoon of margarine, lightly grease two 450g/1lb loaf tins.

2 Heat the oven to 180C/350F/Gas 4.

3 Mix the flour, baking powder, salt, coconut, 175g/6oz sugar and the raisins together in a bowl.

4 Add the egg, evaporated milk, melted margarine and almond essence and mix well together to form a firm dough.

5 Divide the dough into 2 and fill the loaf tins. Mix the remaining sugar with 1 tablespoon of hot water and brush over the loaves.

6 Bake in the centre of the oven for about 1 hour, or until a skewer inserted into the centre of the loaves comes out clean.

7 Leave to cool in the tins, then turn out and serve sliced, and buttered if wished.

Coconut Bread (front) and Gingerbread

Fried Yeast Rolls
Floats

Fried Yeast Rolls, or Floats as they are called in Trinidad, are the traditional accompaniment to a dish called accra, or salt fish cakes. Accra are similar to Stamp and Go (see page 25) but are made with the addition of yeast.

1 teaspoon sugar
1 teaspoon dried yeast
350g/12oz plain flour
1 teaspoon salt
¼ teaspoon cayenne pepper
50g/2oz lard, cut into cubes
5 tablespoons oil

Makes 15

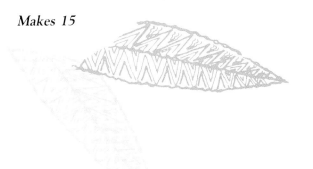

1 Dissolve the sugar in 4 tablespoons of warm water. Sprinkle the yeast into the water and set aside for 10 minutes in a warm place.

2 Put the flour, salt and cayenne pepper into a bowl. Add the lard cubes and rub into the mixture with your fingertips until the mixture resembles very fine breadcrumbs.

3 Add the yeast and enough warm water, about 150ml/¼ pint, to make a soft dough. Knead the dough on a lightly floured surface until it is smooth and elastic. Return to the bowl, cover with a clean tea towel and leave in a warm place for 1½ hours, or until it has doubled in volume.

4 Break off golf-ball size pieces and roll into balls, flouring your hands to prevent the dough sticking. Place on a baking sheet and leave to rise for another 20 minutes. Roll the risen balls out to about 5mm/¼in thick.

5 Heat the oil in a large heavy-based frying-pan and fry, a few at a time, for 2-3 minutes, until cooked inside and golden brown on the outside.

6 Drain on absorbent paper and serve hot.

Cornmeal Dumplings

These popular if rather heavy dumplings are served with many of the more hearty dishes of the Caribbean islands.

100g/4oz plain flour
100g/4oz cornmeal
1 teaspoon baking powder
1 teaspoon salt
1 tablespoon finely chopped fresh chives
40g/1½oz lard, cut into cubes

Makes 24

1 Put the flour, cornmeal, baking powder, salt and chives in a mixing bowl. Add the lard and rub into the mixture with your fingertips until the mixture resembles fine breadcrumbs. Stir in 6 tablespoons of cold water to make a stiff dough. Roll the dough into balls to make dumplings.

2 Bring a large pan of salted water to the boil and drop in the dumplings. Cover the pan, lower the heat slightly and simmer vigorously for 10-15 minutes until dumplings are cooked.

3 Alternatively add the dumplings to a soup or stew and cook as above.

Cheese Corn Sticks
Surullitos

Cheese Corn Sticks, or Surullitos as they are called in Puerto Rico, make a good appetizer to hand round with drinks.

1 teaspoon salt
225g/8oz cornmeal
175g/6oz Edam or Gouda cheese, grated
1 teaspoon paprika
225ml/8fl oz oil

Makes 28-30

1 Pour 700ml/1¼ pints water into a saucepan, add the salt and bring to the boil over moderate heat.

2 Gradually pour the cornmeal into the boiling water, stirring constantly, and cook for 3 minutes until the mixture is thick and smooth.

3 Remove from the heat and stir in the grated cheese and paprika. When the mixture is cool enough to handle, roll into sticks approximately 7.5 ×2.5cm/ 3 × 1in, wetting your hands from time to time to prevent the mixture from sticking.

4 Heat the oil in a medium frying-pan over moderate heat. Fry the sticks a few at a time for 2-3 minutes until golden brown. Remove with a slotted spoon and drain on absorbent paper.

Fried Bread Rolls
Bakes

These Fried Bread Rolls are delicious served hot, split open and spread with butter or filled with Trinidad Fried Shark (see page 25).

Although they are best eaten as soon as they have been cooked, they can be fried an hour before serving and kept warm in a low oven.

900g/2lb plain flour
1 tablespoon salt
1½ tablespoons sugar
5 tablespoons baking powder
75g/3oz butter or margarine, cut into cubes
oil, for deep-frying

Makes 20

1 Put the flour, salt, sugar and baking powder into a large mixing bowl.

2 Add the butter or margarine and rub into the flour with your fingertips until the mixture resembles coarse breadcrumbs.

3 Gradually add 550ml/19fl oz water, until it forms a firm dough. Knead for a few minutes until smooth.

4 Divide into 20 pieces and roll each piece into a ball, using a little flour if necessary. Flatten with a floured rolling pin to about 5mm/¼ in thick and 7.5cm/3in in diameter.

5 Heat 1.5cm/½ in of oil in a deep frying-pan over moderate heat. When the oil is hot, add the doughballs a few at a time. Lower the heat slightly and fry for 5-7 minutes, turning a few times, until golden brown, taking care not to burn them. Remove with a slotted spoon and drain on absorbent paper while frying the remaining dough.

6 Place on a baking sheet and keep warm in a low oven until ready to serve.

DRINKS

Rum-based drinks are synonymous with the Caribbean. It is a liquor that is common to all the islands. There is light rum, golden rum and dark rum, each one with its own taste and character. White rum is ideal for mixing with soft drinks or fruit juices and for making popular cocktails such as Banana Daiquiri (see page 121). Golden rum is my own particular favourite for Rum Punch (see page 120) but it is also excellent for other rum-based drinks such as Cream Punch (see page 120). Dark rum has a heavy molasses flavour and is best used for cooking. And for those people who do not enjoy rum there are endless exotic and thirst-quenching fruit drinks to choose from.

Rum Punch

Every island in the Caribbean has its own version of Rum Punch. Most people follow the general rule of one sour, two sweet, three strong and four weak, though I tend to prefer another version – one sour, two sweet, three strong and no weak!

225g/8oz white sugar
125ml/4fl oz fresh lime juice
350ml/12fl oz golden rum
225ml/8fl oz crushed ice or ice cubes
dash of Angostura bitters
grated nutmeg

Makes 775ml/28fl oz (Serves 4-6)

1 First make the sugar syrup: put the sugar in a small saucepan. Pour in 225ml/8fl oz cold water and bring to the boil over moderate heat, stirring constantly. Lower the heat and simmer for 3-5 minutes, or until the sugar has dissolved and the liquid is clear. Remove from the heat and set aside until the sugar syrup has cooled.

2 When the syrup is completely cold, pour it into a large jug. Then add the lime juice, the golden rum and the crushed ice or ice cubes and mix everything thoroughly together.

3 Pour into 4-6 wine glasses, add a dash of Angostura bitters and sprinkle over the nutmeg. Serve the rum punch immediately.

Cream Punch
Poncho de Crema

Cream Punch or Poncho de Crema is traditionally served at Christmas time in Trinidad. It is a very strong, rich egg nog, served over lots of crushed ice. It is guaranteed to create a festive mood!

1 egg, beaten
grated rind of ½ lime
200ml/7fl oz condensed milk
200ml/7fl oz evaporated milk
350ml/12fl oz golden rum
225ml/8fl oz crushed ice
dash of Angostura bitters
grated nutmeg

Makes 1l/1¾ pints (Serves 6-8)

1 Put the egg, lime rind, condensed milk, evaporated milk and rum into an electric blender and blend at high speed for 30 seconds.

2 Divide the ice between 6-8 wine glasses and pour over the cream punch. Add a dash of Angostura bitters and sprinkle over the nutmeg. Serve the punch immediately.

On previous page, from the left: Rum Swizzle, Banana Daiquiri, Cream Punch, Bentley, Tropical Fruit Punch and Rum Punch

Rum Swizzle

Rum Swizzle is a perfect combination for those who like their cocktails strong but not too sweet.

300ml/½ pint crushed ice
175ml/6fl oz white rum
juice of 2 limes
1 tablespoon caster sugar
2 tablespoons orange-flavoured liqueur

To decorate
2 lime slices
2 cocktail cherries

Makes 2 cocktails

1 Chill 2 cocktail glasses.

2 Put the crushed ice in a cocktail shaker. Pour in the rum, lime juice, sugar and orange-flavoured liqueur. Shake well or swizzle.

3 Strain into the chilled cocktail glasses. Decorate with the lime slices and cherries and serve.

Tropical Fruit Punch

This is a refreshing non-alcoholic drink, full of exotic and tantalizing tastes.

1 large ripe mango, puréed
300ml/½ pint pineapple juice
300ml/½ pint fresh orange juice
150ml/¼ pint fresh lime juice
125ml/4fl oz sugar syrup (see page 120)
4 teaspoons grenadine syrup
chopped pineapple, orange and banana,
to decorate (optional)

Makes 625ml/21fl oz (Serves 4)

1 Put the mango purée, pineapple juice, orange juice, lime juice and sugar syrup in a large jug.

2 Add lots of crushed ice and mix well together with a long spoon. Pour into 4 wine glasses. Add a teaspoon of grenadine to each glass, decorate with the chopped fruit, if liked, and serve immediately.

Bentley – The Teetotaller's Drink

It looks like a cocktail but is made with only lime juice, sugar, soda water and Angostura bitters – a favourite flavouring in many Caribbean drinks.

300ml/½ pint fresh lime juice
4 tablespoons caster sugar
300ml/½ pint soda water
Angostura bitters

Makes 600ml/1 pint (Serves 4)

1 Chill 4 tall glasses.

2 Mix the lime juice with the sugar in a jug, stirring constantly until the sugar has dissolved.

3 Add ice cubes and pour in the soda water. Add Angostura bitters to taste, mix well together and serve in the chilled glasses.

Banana Daiquiri

When frozen Banana Daiquiri is like a banana sorbet – but the after-effects are quite different!

125ml/4fl oz white rum
2 tablespoons caster sugar
75ml/3fl oz fresh lime juice
1 banana, sliced
600ml/1 pint crushed ice
banana slices, to decorate

Makes 2 cocktails

1 Chill 2 cocktail glasses.

2 Put the rum, caster sugar, lime juice, sliced banana and crushed ice into an electric blender and blend at high speed for 30 seconds.

3 Pour into the cocktail glasses and decorate with the banana slices. Serve immediately.

GLOSSARY

Ackee: the fruit of a West African tree brought to Jamaica in the 18th century by Captain Bligh. When ripe the pear-shaped scarlet pod bursts open, exposing the edible cream-coloured aril. Canned ackee is available.

Banana Leaves: used as a wrapping for certain dishes, giving the food a distinctive flavour. Available from some Chinese supermarkets and South-East Asian stores.

Breadfruit: a large round green fruit with a bumpy thick skin. The creamy flesh can be baked, boiled or fried. Available both fresh and canned from West Indian shops.

Christophene: also known as choco, chayote and cho-cho. A pear-shaped squash, it has a delicate flavour and ranges in colour from creamy white to dark green. Widely available fresh or canned from West Indian shops.

Dasheen: a tropical root vegetable, also known as eddo, taro and 'old cocoyam', like a large bark-covered round swede. The leaves are used to make Callaloo. Available from West Indian shops.

Guava: similar to a small quince in appearance with a green, yellow, pink or cream coloured skin and an inner pulp full of small seeds. The ripe fruit can be eaten raw but more often it is made into a compote or 'cheese' (compressed preserve). Widely available.

Mango: a tropical fruit much used in Caribbean cooking. The unripe fruit is used for making chutneys and relishes. When ripe the colour may vary from green to bright red, with a sweet yellow juicy flesh encasing a large seed.

Molasses: a thick liquid residue derivative from sugar cane. Light molasses is used as a table syrup; dark molasses, which has a stronger flavour, is used in cooking for cakes and breads.

Okra: also known as okros, ladies fingers or bamie. A green, slightly hairy pod native to Africa, used to thicken soups, stews and also eaten as a vegetable. Widely available both fresh and canned from West Indian and Asian shops.

Palm Hearts: the terminal buds of a variety of palm trees. These mild-flavoured ivory-coloured shoots are canned and exported throughout the world. Available from delicatessens and West Indian shops.

Pawpaw: also known as papaya. A tropical fruit widely used in Caribbean cooking, similar in appearance to an elongated melon. Unripe, it is cooked as a vegetable or used to make chutneys. Ripe, it is yellow or orange with a soft orange flesh filled with shiny grey or black seeds. It is then eaten raw like a melon with a squeeze of lime juice.

Peppers: it is the hot seasoning peppers that give Caribbean cooking its distinctive flavour. Care should be taken when handling them: do not touch your face or eyes after working with them and be sure to wash your hands thoroughly. They resemble small sweet peppers (see picture on page 94) and are available from West Indian shops. Chillies can be substituted but for a more authentic flavour add a dash of bottled pepper sauce.

Pigeon Peas: used in soups, stews or as a vegetable with rice. Available fresh, dried and canned from West Indian shops.

Plantain: like a large banana but without the sweetness. It must be cooked before it is eaten. Sold in varying stages of ripeness from green to almost black. Available from West Indian or Asian shops.

Salt Cod: used in many of the traditional Caribbean dishes. Available on the bone or filleted and wrapped in plastic packets, from West Indian and some Italian shops.

Shaddock: the largest member of the citrus fruit family, introduced to the Caribbean from Polynesia. It has a thick rind and juicy bitter flesh, like a bitter grapefruit. It is thought the grapefruit evolved from the shaddock.

Sweet Potato: a starchy vegetable native to tropical America. The skin varies in colour from brown to pink to white and the flesh also varies from orange to white. Available from ethnic stores and some supermarkets.

Tannia: also known as yautia or 'new cocoyam'. A starchy root vegetable similar to the dasheen.

Topi Tambo: a tropical root vegetable with a texture similar to water chestnut.

Yam: a tuberous root and one of the staple vegetables of the Caribbean. It comes in various shapes, with a bark-like skin and creamy yellow flesh which has a nutty flavour. Potatoes can be used as a substitute.

INDEX